HOW TO MAKE A NEW MOTHER HAPPY

How to Make a
New Mother
Happy

A Doctor's Guide to Solving Her Most Common Problems— Quickly and Effectively

by Uzzi Reiss, M.D., OB/GYN & Yfat M. Reiss

CHRONICLE BOOKS
SAN FRANCISCO

OTHER BOOKS BY UZZI REISS, M.D., OB/GYN:

How to Make a Pregnant Woman Happy: A Doctor's Guide to Solving Pregnancy's Most Common Problems—Quickly and Effectively, with Yfat M. Reiss

Natural Hormone Balance for Women: Look Younger, Feel Stronger, and Live Life with Exuberance, with Martin Zucker

Library of Congress Cataloging-in-Publication Data available.

ISBN: 0-8118-4205-3

Manufactured in Canada.

Designed by Pamela Geismar

Distributed in Canada by Raincoast Books
9050 Shaughnessy Street
Vancouver, British Columbia V6P 6E5

10 9 8 7 6 5 4 3 2 1

Chronicle Books LLC
85 Second Street
San Francisco, California 94105

www.chroniclebooks.com

This book is dedicated to our family and friends, who supported us through the happy and sometimes challenging labor and delivery stages of the writing of this book, and to the many new mothers who assisted and inspired us to make them happy.

We extend a special thank-you to Yael Reiss, the wife and mother we both hope to make happiest of all.

✳ ✳ ✳

CONTENTS

Part Two: THE NEW MOTHER'S MIND:
RECOGNIZING, PREVENTING & TREATING POSTPARTUM
DEPRESSION & MOOD CHANGES

Part Three: THE NEW MOTHER'S LIFE:
THE CHALLENGES OF BALANCING BABY, SELF & PARTNER

How to Use This Book

Got a problem? Simply look up the problem or symptoms in the table of contents or index of this guidebook and go to the page that addresses that problem.

That's it.

No need to read the book from cover to cover. This guidebook is designed for use by busy men and women on an as-needed basis. Each solution in this book is organized as follows:

THE PROBLEM:
   The name of the problem or symptom

THE FACTS:
   A brief explanation of why this problem occurs

WHAT YOU CAN DO:
   A listing of simple remedies you can use to make a new mother feel better

WHEN TO GET MORE HELP:
   A listing of symptoms that should be referred to her physician

You now know all you need to make a new mother happy.

INTRODUCTION

This guidebook is written for men and women who want answers to the questions and problems that come with new motherhood. If you're looking for an easy way to adjust to the many changes and challenges a new family faces, then this book is for you.

How to Make a New Mother Happy is designed to make it easy for busy men to be attentive new fathers and for busy, exhausted women to find the solutions they need in order to enjoy their time as new mothers. Simply look up your question or the symptom in the table of contents or the index and turn to the section on your topic. You'll find a brief explanation of why the problem occurs, a list of easy actions you can take to be helpful, and a description of those symptoms that warrant a call to a physician. *That's it.*

Ideally, expectant mothers and fathers will peruse this guidebook prior to delivery and then refer to it on an as-needed basis after delivery. New fathers may choose to keep a copy with them in case their partner calls with a problem when they're at work or on the go—that way they can always be helpful, even by telephone.

How to Make a New Mother Happy gives you quick, easy, and effective ways to show her that you are engaged and involved without having to read pages and pages of dense text.

A Tool for Couples

This book aims to arm new mothers and fathers with tools for tackling the tough issues that come up during those challenging first few months, which are often called the "postpartum" period, or the "fourth trimester." There is no one "right" answer to any given problem. This guidebook offers several approaches that have worked for other couples. Which remedies should you implement? The answer is highly personal. Each remedy you adopt must work for your baby, but it must also work for *you, your partner,* and *your family as a whole.* A solution that works for the baby only is no solution at all and will eventually become too burdensome to be helpful.

The goal of this guidebook is to help you give your child something that has become rare—a happy and intact family led by two parents who continue to enjoy each other even while facing the challenges of caring for a new baby. How can you increase your baby's chances of enjoying such a strong, happy family? By being your baby's advocate and insisting that the decisions you make for him or her work for the mother, father, and family around him. As a result you will strengthen the bond between you.

Treating Physical Discomforts Following Delivery

The first section of this guidebook is designed to provide easy home remedies for typical physical problems and discomforts that are common right after delivery. Reading about physical discomforts may make some new fathers uneasy, but you may ultimately find it reassuring to have clear information about what you can do to make your partner feel better and what symptoms should prompt you to call her physician.

In his thirty years as an obstetrician and gynecologist, Dr. Reiss has focused on finding natural and nutritional alternatives to prescription medication. For this reason this guidebook proposes hundreds of natural home remedies. Vitamins, minerals, and simple changes in diet can go a long way toward making a new mother happier, healthier, and more energetic.

However, while it may be beneficial to use these simple, natural remedies whenever possible, this book is not intended to replace regular obstetric care. Encourage your partner to consult her physician before using any of the supplements or suggestions outlined in this guidebook.

Postpartum Depression & Mood Changes

Nearly 80 percent of women experience some form of mood change after delivery. At a time that should be joyous, many women—and their partners—find that they are struck by sadness or irritability. But they don't have to be. Postpartum mood changes can be prevented and treated by implementing lifestyle, nutritional, and hormonal solutions. The second section of this book is devoted to explaining this condition and offering couples specific instructions for preventing and treating it—*together.*

New Parents' New Reality

Becoming a parent requires a great deal of adjustment. Many couples find themselves wondering what has become of their "old life" and the intimacy they once enjoyed. New parenthood needn't be this way. The final section of this guidebook addresses the various lifestyle challenges facing new parents—getting enough sleep, finding child care, tackling housework, and social-izing—and provides specific suggestions that will help your family work around these logistics.

When to Call Her Physician

Many new parents are reluctant to call the physician when a problem arises; no one wants to be a "high maintenance" patient.

Unfortunately, they've got it all wrong. Physicians aren't psychic; they require a partnership between themselves and their patient in order to provide the very best care. And almost every physician would rather get a call at two o'clock in the morning, when something can still be done, than hours later at nine in the morning, when it's too late to solve the problem and he or she has a waiting room full of patients. So be a savvy consumer of health-care services. The next time your partner visits her physician, encourage her to ask, "What symptoms or problems should cause me to call you immediately, night or day?" With this knowledge, you and your partner will never feel uncomfortable about calling, and you won't put off getting help with a problem that requires immediate attention.

Later, when one of you calls the physician regarding a specific problem or concern, always end the conversation by asking, "What symptoms should cause me to call you again?" Then you'll always know when to make a follow-up call.

You'll notice that some of the "What You Can Do" sections of this guidebook recommend that you call her physician regarding a specific symptom or test. In making this suggestion, it is assumed that you and your partner have both agreed to make the call or that your partner is not able to make the call herself. Keep in mind that your partner may feel embarrassed, uncomfortable, or angry if you contact her physician without her consent, so make sure to discuss the situation with her before placing the call.

Know Your Partner

This guidebook provides a number of suggestions for each common problem or symptom that may arise during the first few months of new motherhood. Does this mean that every time she expresses discomfort you should bombard her with advice? Not necessarily.

You know your partner best. If she usually prefers to hear just one helpful piece of advice, then go through each suggestion to determine which one might appeal to her. On the other hand, if she likes to be very informed, read the various treatment and prevention options and decide together. Never badger her to confirm that she has followed through. Finally, remember that your most helpful action during her first few months as a mother may turn out to be almost no action at all—just a supportive word and a little "sick day" treatment.

The New Mother's
Body

Delivery-Related Physical Challenges & Their Solutions

RECOVERY AFTER DELIVERY

1

What Happens Now?!? Preparing for the Arrival of Your Baby

The Facts:

Your baby has arrived! It's beautiful. It's perfect. Are *you* ready?

This book is a tool for couples. Many expectant mothers and fathers discuss how they will work together *during* labor—sometimes creating a birthing plan—but couples rarely speak about what will happen in the moment their baby *arrives*.

What will the new father do in the minutes after delivery? Should he stay with his partner? Should he follow the new baby? Should he put down the camera? Should he step aside? And if all isn't going as planned, where will he be most helpful?

What You Can Do:

Although not meant to be a comprehensive listing of the many considerations following delivery, the following will prepare expectant couples and help both new mother and father act as a team in the minutes and hours after delivery:

* Mothers and fathers need time to bond with their baby as early as possible. Babies are extremely alert and highly sensitive to the contact they receive in the first few hours of life. As such, advocating the need for you and your partner to have *physical* contact with your new baby is paramount.

* Although mothers and fathers look forward to bonding with their baby in these first hours, the reality is that some couples are simply too exhausted or are otherwise unable to do so following delivery. Take time to consider who can assist you and the new mother during this time if neither of you are available for your baby. A grandparent, sibling, or trusted friend will be far more attentive to your baby than a nurse (who must attend

to many babies). Discuss who would be able to "pinch-hit" if the need arises.

* Consider other possibilities:

    ⊙ What if your baby requires immediate medical attention and must be transferred to the pediatric unit?

    ⊙ What if the new mother requires immediate medical attention?

    ⊙ What if both require medical attention?

Discuss these possibilities with your partner ahead of time. Because she may be unable to act, it is important that you understand her wishes and preferences. Allow her to dictate what will be your role in any of these situations. Should you stay and "track" your baby? Should you stay with your partner? The reality is that you cannot be in two places at once, or you may be unavailable for whatever reason. And if you are unavailable, who can assist you in tracking your new baby *and* being supportive to your exhausted partner? Choosing a family member or friend in advance can be incredibly helpful during an already stressful time.

* On the other hand, help your partner balance her natural desire to bond with her new baby with her need for rest. Encourage her to designate someone whom she trusts enough to be with the baby while she sleeps.

When to Get More Help:
Take the time to discuss the hours after delivery with friends and family who have recently given birth. Take these stories into account in your "post-birthing plan."

Sneak a peak at the third section of this guidebook, "The New Mother's Life: The Challenges of Balancing Baby, Self & Partner," for additional considerations for your larger "post-birthing plan."

A New Mother's General State after Delivery

The Facts:

In the days and weeks that follow the birth of your baby, a new mother's body and mind go through significant changes. With nearly every one of these physical and emotional challenges, your assistance and acknowledgment will go a long way toward making her feel better and recover more quickly. A new mother is likely to:

- ⊙ feel fatigued

- ⊙ feel concerned

- ⊙ feel pain

- ⊙ feel elated, overwhelmed, and frightened

- ⊙ feel frustrated or confused

- ⊙ feel sad

What You Can Do:

* A new mother is likely to feel tired both from the physically challenging delivery process and from sleep deprivation associated with caring for a newborn. See "Fatigue & Exhaustion" (page 72) and "Sleep Deprivation & Insomnia" (page 76) for more information on helping her deal with fatigue.

* A new mother experiences exhaustion, weakness, pain, and bleeding while recovering from the delivery and any procedures she underwent during the delivery. See "Postpartum Bleeding & Discharge" (page 25), "Postpartum Cramping" (page 28), and "Caring for Tears & Cuts" (page 30) for more information on easing her recovery process.

* A new mother often feels extreme elation over the arrival of her baby, but she may also feel concerned about the health of her baby and whether she can properly care for her newborn. See "Mild Mood Swings, Including Mild Anxiety & Depression" (page 81) for more information on helping her deal with her feelings.

* A new mother may feel frustrated by the process of learning to breastfeed and may experience physical breastfeeding complications. See chapter 5, "Breastfeeding," in this guidebook for more information on how to help her handle breastfeeding challenges.

* A new mother is often concerned about her appearance. Once her baby is out, she may be dismayed by abdominal skin that doesn't instantly snap back into shape. See "Changes in Her Abdominal Area" (page 163) for more information on helping her feel better about her body and take care of herself so she can get back in shape.

* A new mother may feel sad about the extreme changes in her life. Some of her sadness may be related to hormonal changes. See "Mild Postpartum Depression or 'Baby Blues'" (page 182) for more information on how to help her work through her feelings of sadness or depression.

* If your partner's delivery was aided by an epidural, she was likely given a catheter that remained in place for up to twenty-four hours after delivery, which presents a risk for bladder infection similar to those suffered by women who use a catheter during a C-section. For more information on this, see the section on bladder infections in "Caring for C-Section Wounds" (page 48).

? With all of this going on, what can you do to make your partner feel better? Surprisingly, simply keeping her company, listening to her, ensuring that she eats well and gets as much rest as possible, pampering her, and being involved in the baby's care help more than you can imagine.

Receiving excellent care in the first few days, especially in the days right after coming home from the hospital, can really make a difference in a new mother's feelings of well-being and competence. New fathers can help in this regard by anticipating and meeting her physical and emotional needs and keeping the household running while she recovers. Arranging for extra help with household chores such as laundry, cleaning, and grocery shopping, and providing extra help with caring for older children are essential. See chapter 9, "Resuming Your Life Together," in this guidebook for more information.

When to Get More Help:

Luckily, new fathers needn't reinvent the wheel when learning how to be a helpful partner. Simply paging through this guidebook will arm you with a great deal of information. When in doubt, consult with family, friends with young children, or your partner's physician for more information.

Postpartum Bleeding & Discharge

The Facts:

After a woman gives birth, vaginal bleeding and discharge of pregnancy-related uterine tissue continue for up to six weeks after the delivery. This natural process occurs regardless of whether the baby was delivered vaginally or by C-section. During the first six weeks or so, a new mother can expect the following:

- ⊙ **Day 1 to 10:** heavy, bright-red bleeding and discharge of blood clots

- ⊙ **Day 11 to 20:** bleeding that appears more brownish in color, with occasional episodes of bright-red bleeding

- ⊙ **Day 21 to 45:** thinner, lighter, less frequent discharge, composed mostly of mucous that is pinkish in color and rarely bloody

- ⊙ **After 45 days:** All discharge should end about six weeks following delivery.

What You Can Do:

- ✳ As a couple, discuss whether breastfeeding is appropriate for your family; breastfeeding causes uterine contractions, the mechanism by which the uterus expels the tissue related to the pregnancy, decreases blood loss, and returns the uterus to its normal size.

- ✳ If she so desires, assist your partner in massaging her uterus from the outside. Although it may sound strange, massaging the uterus helps a new mother's body remove the materials of the pregnancy, particularly if performed frequently in the first week following delivery. Uterine massages are especially beneficial for new mothers who are not breastfeeding. To perform a uterine massage, take all four fingers and push deeply below the navel, or belly button. Keep pushing down until your hand feels the dome of the uterus, and then begin massaging in a circular motion. Ask one of your partner's labor and delivery nurses for direct instruction on this. Your partner's abdomen and uterus will be

very tender and painful during the first few days, so comply with her request if she asks you to stop or adjust your technique. Generally, this massage is not required beyond the second week following delivery.

? Why is it helpful to massage a new mother's uterus?
During the late stages of pregnancy, the uterus grows to many times its nonpregnant size—spanning from the pelvis to the rib cage. Once a new mother delivers, the uterus changes from a soft and spongy mass to a hard ball of tissue. You can feel this "hard ball" if you press your fingers down between your partner's navel and her pubic bone (ask for her permission before you do this, of course). Massaging the uterus causes it to contract and expel pregnancy-related tissue from your partner's body. See "Postpartum Cramping" (page 28) for more information.

When to Get More Help:

Any continuous heavy bleeding or passing of blood clots after the first ten days following delivery should be brought to the attention of your partner's physician. The following conditions may make your partner more susceptible to heavy bleeding and should be brought to the attention of her physician (*even if you believe he or she is already be aware of the condition*):

- ⊙ a larger baby

- ⊙ a prolonged labor

- ⊙ a labor that required medication to induce full labor

- ⊙ infection during labor that required antibiotic treatment

- ⊙ placental tissue that was not removed following delivery and still requires removal

Any time your partner believes she is bleeding more than is normal, you or she may contact her physician and request an evaluation of your partner's hemoglobin, hematocrit, and iron levels.

A new mother may experience increased bleeding if she overuses pain relievers such as aspirin or ibuprofen. In this event, you or she may want to contact her physician for an evaluation and an alternative pain management program.

Postpartum Cramping

The Facts:

When a new mother experiences cramping following her delivery, she is actually feeling the same uterine contractions that helped her deliver her baby. Why is her uterus still contracting? It does this in order to slow and eventually stop the bleeding that is common after delivery and to return to its normal size.

In the first seven to ten days following childbirth, a new mother will experience heavy bleeding and strong contractions, which feel like intense menstrual cramps. The more pregnancies your partner has had, the stronger these contractions and cramping may feel. These contractions become even more intense when she breastfeeds, since the baby's sucking on her nipple causes a woman's body to produce *oxytocin*, the hormone that helps produce milk and cause the uterus to contract.

Women who give birth by C-section experience the same quantity and intensity of postpartum contractions; however, these new mothers may feel more discomfort due to additional pain associated with their incision.

Generally, cramping will begin to decrease after the third week following delivery and will no longer be noticeable by six weeks following delivery. Few women experience severe cramping that continues into the third week and requires pain medication.

What You Can Do:

* In order to ease (but not stop) your partner's contractions, she might ask her physician about supplementing her diet with magnesium glycinate, magnesium gluconate, magnesium cit-rate, magnesium aspartate, or other fast-absorbing magnesium available from your local health food store. Magnesium relaxes the uterus and eases her contractions, but not so much that it

stops contracting and increases bleeding (a problem with other contraction relaxants). She should take the suggested dosage with food and slowly increase her intake every few days until her contractions weaken. She should reduce her dosage if she experiences fatigue, muscle weakness, or diarrhea.

* To avoid *increasing* her contractions, your partner should avoid taking calcium supplements, including stomach aids that contain calcium, such as Tums or Rolaids, since calcium will promote uterine contractions and cramping.

    * Pick up a heating pad or hot water bottle for your partner. If she needs help, assist her in applying it to her lower abdominal area.

    * Keep in mind that massaging your partner's uterus after delivery (to help her body expel the pregnancy materials) will increase contractions and possibly exacerbate the pain of cramping. See "Postpartum Bleeding & Discharge" (page 25) for more information on uterine massage.

* Ibuprofen may be used to reduce pain. Ibuprofen and other anti-inflammatory medications that do not contain narcotics are safe for use while breastfeeding. For more information on taking pain medications while breastfeeding, see the "Use of Pain Medication" (page 60) section in this guidebook.

When to Get More Help:

If your partner's postpartum contractions are severe, and common measures and medications don't help, call her physician. Experiencing pain won't make her a better mother, and seeking the assistance of her physician is unlikely to involve a complicated treatment that would separate her from her baby.

Caring for Tears & Cuts

The Facts:

It is common for a woman delivering a baby vaginally to tear not only in the area of the vagina but also in the perineum, the area between the vagina and the rectum. Often, doctors preemptively cut the perineum in a procedure called an *episiotomy,* in order to prevent more destructive tearing during the pushing stage of delivery. In some cases the episiotomy can extend into the rectum; in others the action of pushing out the baby can cause a tear into the muscle of the rectum. A rectal tear known as a *fourth degree laceration* occurs when the *inner* lining of the rectum is inadvertently cut during the episiotomy procedure or tears during the delivery stage of labor.

A vaginal tear or episiotomy cut should not prevent a new mother from resuming activity as soon as she feels ready to, unless the activity or any associated movement causes discomfort or may re-tear the affected area. Rectal tears are serious business, causing more complications than nearly any other condition that occurs around delivery. This wound is very sensitive to pressure, which means that a just-stitched rectum may not tolerate a hard bowel movement.

What You Can Do:

PREVENTION:

Some new mothers emerge from delivery having had no vaginal tearing and no need for preemptive cutting, but many do not, due to the sometimes incompatible sizes of mothers' pelvises and babies' heads. To avoid vaginal tearing and the need for an episiotomy, consider the following:

* Before delivery, encourage your partner to ask her physician about the type of episiotomy he or she favors. Many doctors perform a *median* or *midline* episiotomy—where the cut begins

at the bottom of the vagina and extends to the top of the rec-tum—as opposed to a *mediolateral* episiotomy—where the cut begins at the bottom of the vagina and extends to the side. A mediolateral episiotomy is more painful while healing but is less likely to cut or cause a tear into the muscle of the rectum and the rectum itself. Many hospitals offer perineal massage during the pushing stage of labor in order to gently relax and stretch the perineum in an effort to avoid an episiotomy. If your partner's obstetrician is comfortable performing a per-ineal massage and/or mediolateral episiotomy (should one become necessary), you and your partner can ask him or her to note this preference in your partner's medical chart and advise the other physicians who may end up delivering your partner in the event your chosen obstetrician is unavailable. Also, you might want to remind the delivering physician of this prefer-ence at the time of delivery.

* Prior to and during delivery, encourage your partner to push in a "controlled" fashion. What is "controlled" pushing? Many women equate this to the kind of control one exercises when lifting and lowering weights during a workout. Rather than pushing up with abandon, the person extends and retracts the arms or legs in a controlled fashion, making for a better mus-cle workout and leading to fewer injuries. This same principle may be applied to the pushing stage of labor. In order to learn how to do controlled pushing—and pick up a great deal of information about how to navigate the entire labor and deliv-ery process as a couple—take a birthing class through the hos-pital in which you and your partner plan to deliver. Then practice the techniques you learn until you both feel comfort-able with them.

TREATMENT:

* Although the thought of wounds in your partner's genital area may make you cringe, you'll be relieved to learn that their loca-tion is actually ideal for healing. The body most effectively

heals wounds in areas with a large blood supply; the vaginal area has a great deal of blood flow and therefore enjoys a relatively quick healing time.

* Of course, in order to help her body do its job, you and she will need to maximize those things that promote healing, like maintaining good nutrition, getting extra rest, and drinking additional water (a new mother should drink approximately eight to twelve glasses of water per day, and more if she is breastfeeding). This regimen will also help prevent complications such as infection and dehydration from arising.

* The new mother should keep the vaginal area clean in order to avoid infection. This can be easily done by rinsing the area with clean water after using the toilet—no soap is needed. Many hospitals also provide new mothers with plastic squirt bottles for filling with warm water to assist them in keeping the vaginal area clean. Your partner will want to be gentle with these bottles to avoid irritating this sensitive area.

* For vaginal tears and cuts, your partner will probably find that she feels well enough to return to some of her normal activities within one week to ten days. She may do so, *as long as she takes care not to aggravate her wound for six weeks after delivery.* For example, new mothers with vaginal tears or episiotomy cuts should refrain from engaging in physical activity or exercises that require them to spread their legs wide, as is often done while doing stretching, yoga, and other popular wellness activities.

- For anal tears and cuts, encourage your partner to aggressively avoid constipation, since this malady produces a wide and dry stool that may re-tear the rectum. Make sure the hospital staff sends your partner home with a variety of constipation-preventing medications or supplements generally available only to hospitals and physicians. You or she should speak to her physician about this while she is still in the hospital, especially if she was prone to constipation before or during her pregnancy. On the other hand, gently remind your partner not to overuse constipation preventatives and remedies, as this may cause diarrhea, which might put undue strain on her bowels.

When to Get More Help:

Some sutures are designed to automatically dissolve within a week or a few months. Ask you partner's physician what to expect from the type of sutures used in her procedure. If her sutures cause discomfort, after the first few weeks you might suggest that she speak to her physician about having the sutures removed prior to the time they are designed to dissolve. The tissue may actually heal before the sutures dissolve.

If the healing seems to stop, if your partner feels increased pain, or if redness or swelling appears in the area of the tear, you or she should contact her physician to rule out or treat infection. If your partner's physician explains that he or she does not need to see your partner and instead prescribes pain medication, insist that she be seen in order to rule out infection in the tear or cut, which can easily be treated with antibiotics when detected early.

In the case of rectal tears and cuts, you or she should contact her physician if your partner develops a fever, has gas or feces coming from her vagina, or experiences increased pain or swelling of the rectal area.

Water Retention: Swollen Feet, Ankles & Hands

The Facts:

Water retention, or edema, is extremely common immediately after delivery. Why? In the weeks leading up to delivery, your partner's body begins accumulating a reserve of water in anticipation of her inability to eat and drink during labor. Considering that some labors last several days and involve the loss of body fluids, the reserved water allows the baby and mother to remain relatively hydrated. While water retention is a lifesaving evolutionary solution, it is unnecessary in our contemporary society.

This potentially lifesaving function can become a nuisance during pregnancy when the additional fluid collects in the "soft tissue" areas of the body, such as the hands and ankles. This condition becomes *more* dramatic immediately following delivery, when the extra fluid that once supported the baby and the uterus is redirected to the soft tissue areas of the body, such as the hands and feet.

? Why does fluid collect in the hands, ankles, and feet? Actually, fluid collects in soft tissue throughout the body, but gravity causes fluid to "pool" in the lowest parts of a woman's extremities, her hands and feet.

This accumulation of fluid will increase every day during the first week after delivery, but it should begin to decrease after the first week. Within three to four weeks, most new mothers find that their water retention has significantly subsided. By six weeks after delivery, most women have shed nearly all of the excess water, due to an increase in urination, night sweats, and daytime perspiration. Unfortunately, dealing with all of this excess fluid can be an uncomfortable experience for the new mom. While retaining water she feels bloated, clumsy, and stiff, and while expelling water she sweats and wakes up frequently to run to the bathroom. Despite all this, water retention should not prevent her from engaging in the activities she feels that she can handle.

? How can a woman tell if she is retaining water? She can push her index finger against the bone of her ankle. If her finger creates an indentation that takes a few seconds to fade, then she has edema. Performing this test regularly is a good way for her to monitor her edema.

What You Can Do:

Providing help for swollen hands and feet involves taking action to reduce the swelling and make her more comfortable.

BRING DOWN HER SWELLING:

* Encourage her to supplement her diet with magnesium glycinate, magnesium gluconate, magnesium citrate, magnesium aspartate, or other fast-absorbing magnesium available from your local health food store. She should take the suggested dosage with food and slowly increase her intake every few days until her swelling decreases, for up to six weeks. She should reduce her dosage if she experiences fatigue, muscle weakness, or diarrhea. Magnesium is safe for use when breastfeeding.

* If your partner is taking magnesium, she might consider adding vitamin B complex to her supplement program. A dosage of 25 to 50 milligrams per day will increase the efficiency of her magnesium supplement and will also boost her energy level. She can also try 100 milligrams of vitamin B_6 twice daily. Vitamin B_6 is a natural diuretic.

* Evening primrose oil capsules with the active ingredient gamma linolenic acid, available in your health food store, can help reduce your partner's swelling. A dose containing 125 milligrams of gamma linolenic acid should be taken with breakfast. Evening primrose oil is safe for use when breastfeeding.

- Make your partner a salad or smoothie that includes parsley, cilantro, dill, cucumber, green pepper, asparagus, watermelon, or dandelion leaves. All of these are natural diuretics and are helpful in reducing water retention.

- Encourage your partner to lie down and relax. Lying in a horizontal position promotes the reabsorption of the retained water. Of course, she won't take this advice unless you're caring for the baby while she's taking a break. Offer to watch the baby, so that she feels comfortable taking a moment for herself.

- Draw a warm bath for your partner. Take care of the baby or arrange for someone else to do so while she soaks. Immersing her entire body in the water will help move fluid away from her extremities while giving her a much-deserved break from an overwhelming first week as a mother.

- Unless otherwise indicated by her physician, a woman does not need to restrict salt consumption simply because she is retaining water. Sodium should be restricted only when water retention increases immediately after she eats salty food.

MAKE HER MORE COMFORTABLE:

- Encourage her to wear loose-fitting clothing.

- You might suggest that she purchase or borrow larger athletic shoes rather than squeezing into ill-fitting shoes or wearing slip-ons. Winter weather can cause walkways to become slippery in some parts of the world, and navigation can be challenging for a new mother, who is unaccustomed to carrying her newly nonpregnant body along with a new little body. Suggest that she purchase new shoes prior to her delivery, or purchase them for her. Although your partner may prefer thongs, slip-ons, or other shoes that don't confine her feet, athletic shoes that provide ankle support and traction are best.

Purchase a size that fits her now, regardless of whether she will be able to wear them after her feet return to their pre-pregnancy size. Alternatively, she might want to borrow athletic shoes from your closet, or from a friend. Note that your partner's level of water retention will rise and fall very quickly. The shoes she wore yesterday may not fit her today.

* If your partner's hands and fingers swell, she may choose to remove her rings until after her swelling decreases.

When to Get More Help:

If your partner's water retention is accompanied by headache, blurry vision, pain below the sternum (where she would feel heartburn), decreased urination, or red or dark urine, call her physician immediately. Your partner should be examined in order to rule out the rare condition postpartum toxemia, an elevation of blood pressure that may be related to kidney and liver dysfunction.

Hemorrhoids

The Facts:

It is common for new mothers to suffer from hemorrhoids after their delivery. Why? During the last stages of labor, women are required to push—putting a great deal of pressure on the vascular system in and around the rectum—resulting in bulging and painful irritation of this area. New mothers are more likely to suffer from hemorrhoids after delivery if they were prone to hemorrhoids, constipation, or varicose veins (a related condition) before or during their pregnancy.

It is important for you, the new father, to understand that this condition is extremely unpleasant—*particularly* when coupled with other postpartum challenges.

What You Can Do:

PREVENTION:

* Throughout her pregnancy, help her avoid constipation at all costs. See "Constipation" (page 160) for more information.

* Encourage your partner to stay hydrated. New mothers should drink eight to twelve glasses of water per day (and even more if she is breastfeeding), a practice that will help ward off both constipation and hemorrhoids.

TREATMENT:

* To bring down swelling, visit your local pharmacy for zinc and zinc oxide creams and other over-the-counter hemorrhoid treatment products such as hemorrhoidal pads with witch hazel. Your partner should apply to the affected area as directed.

* A sitz bath may help bring down swelling and irritation. Assist your partner by drawing her a shallow bath of hot water and adding a generous amount of Epsom salt. Encourage her to soak in the sitz bath for ten to fifteen minutes twice daily.

* Visit your local health food store for other natural anti-inflammatory remedies, including fish-oil capsules that contain both EPA and DHA. Encourage your partner to take fish-oil capsules containing 2 to 3 grams of docosahexaenoic acid (DHA) and eicosapentaenoic acid (EPA), twice daily, 900 milligrams of curcumin (made from the turmeric spice) twice daily, or a digestive enzyme that includes bromelain as directed. Fish-oil capsules, curcumin, and bromelain are all safe for use when breastfeeding.

* Only the worst cases of hemorrhoids will cause new mothers to seek prescriptive pain relief. Your partner will want to avoid pain relievers containing opiates, such as Vicodin, codeine, Percocet, and Darvocet. These narcotics are highly addictive; they tend to increase constipation, thereby exacerbating her hemorrhoids; and they cause sedation, reducing her ability to care for her newborn. Instead, she may choose to take a higher dosage of ibuprofen, a highly effective pain reliever that also functions as an anti-inflammatory. She can take up to 800 milligrams three times daily with her physician's approval.

! A new mother should not use suppositories or insert anything into her rectum if she sustained third- or fourth-
degree lacerations during her delivery. See "Caring for
Tears & Cuts" (page 30) for more information.

When to Get More Help:

If your partner experiences constant pain that does not respond
to the remedies suggested above, contact her physician for a
referral to a gastroenterologist or colon surgeon. Thrombosed
hemorrhoid, a common complication of hemorrhoids, requires
additional medical attention in order to alleviate pain. If your
partner's physician only suggests pain medication, encourage her
to insist on receiving a referral to rule out this condition.

Blood Loss after Delivery & Anemia

The Facts:

New mothers lose a significant amount of blood immediately after delivery, which brings down their iron levels. In addition, a new mother's levels of folic acid and vitamins B_{12} and C run low. As a result, anemia and fatigue can set in after delivery. New mothers generally require six weeks to three months in order to regain the blood lost after delivery.

What You Can Do:

PREVENTION:

* Your partner may want to store 2 units of her own blood during her pregnancy. In the event that a blood transfusion is necessary, this blood may be used to boost her blood level prior to her discharge from the hospital. Blood contamination would not be an issue if she stored her own blood.

* Throughout her pregnancy, your partner should supplement her diet with folic acid and vitamins B_{12} and C.

* Iron supplements should be taken during pregnancy only if your partner's iron and iron storage, called *ferritin*, are low. Excessive supplementation of iron in pregnancy may lead to increased incidence of toxemia during pregnancy. However, after significant blood loss, many women will require iron supplements.

TREATMENT:

* Rebuilding red blood cells requires proper nutrition that includes healthy fats and protein. See "Ideal Postpartum Diet" (page 148) for more information.

* Your partner should take a vitamin B_{12} supplement in chewable form, 1 milligram twice daily; folic acid, 1 milligram twice daily; and vitamin C, 1,000 milligrams twice daily.

* She should also supplement her iron intake. Most iron supplements cause indigestion and constipation (see "Constipation," page 160). The more gentle forms of iron supplements are attached to protein and are therefore absorbed more easily by the body. Many of the iron supplements found in health food stores are gentle but are not absorbed well and are therefore less effective. Instead, visit your local pharmacy and pick up Slow Fe pills; your partner can take one pill twice daily, for no more than six weeks.

* Many women are sent home severely anemic and fatigued in order to avoid a blood transfusion. In the future, it's likely that red blood cell builder medication (the same medication that is administered to chemotherapy patients) will be prescribed to women that have experienced substantial blood loss. Such treatment will dramatically enhance recovery. Talk to your physician about this treatment.

When to Get More Help:

If your partner feels extremely tired after delivery and does not attribute this fatigue to the physical and mental trauma of childbirth or to lack of sleep, encourage her to ask her physician to run a full blood panel that includes an analysis of her iron levels, iron storage, red blood cell count, B_{12}, and folic acid level.

Broken Blood Vessels in the Face

The Facts:

The intensity of pushing in labor puts a great deal of pressure on the veins throughout the body, which often results in broken blood vessels on a new mother's face and eyeballs. Often this looks like conjunctivitis, a common eye infection.

What You Can Do:

* If your partner discovers broken blood vessels on her face and eyeballs, reassure her that this is a normal and temporary condition, which will clear up on its own within ten days.

* To reduce broken blood vessels in the face and generally promote healing, an expectant mother should use the sublingual (under the tongue) form of arnica three times a day for the week leading up to her due date. During labor, arnica can be taken every few hours. Then, in the first week following her delivery, the new mother may take arnica every two to four hours and then reduce this to three times a day from the second to sixth weeks following the birth of her baby. Note: Because it is not swallowed, sublingual medication is not considered "food" for purposes of restricting food during labor.

* Your partner is likely to be very self-conscious about her appearance, so never allow her to sense that you are concerned about the way she looks. Reassure her that she is beautiful.

When to Get More Help:

If your partner is concerned about the condition of her eyes and she believes that her condition is severe, encourage her to contact her physician for an evaluation.

Hearing Loss Immediately Following Delivery

The Facts:

In extremely rare cases, new mothers experience mild, moderate, or severe hearing loss in the first few days after delivery. This type of hearing loss, whether continuous or intermittent, should be evaluated immediately by an ear, nose, and throat physician *and* an otologist, a physician who specializes in hearing. The cause of this condition is not well understood. Early diagnosis and prompt treatment are required to prevent permanent hearing loss.

What You Can Do:

* This condition requires immediate evaluation and aggressive treatment. A delay in proper diagnosis and treatment may cause permanent hearing loss. Report the symptoms of this condition to your partner's physician and ensure that she receives care immediately.

* Be your partner's advocate. Don't accept a "wait and see" answer. Insist on an immediate evaluation by an ear, nose, and throat specialist and otologist.

When to Get More Help:

Consult your partner's physician if she experiences any hearing loss after giving birth.

Bathing after Delivery

The Facts:

The vaginal area or C-section incision requires very gentle treatment after your baby is born. These areas were very recently operated on, cut, torn, or stretched and are now in the process of healing. They are likely to be more sensitive than they have been at any other time. When it comes to bathing and cleaning, it is imperative that care is taken not to further irritate them as they heal.

What You Can Do:

AFTER VAGINAL DELIVERY WITH OR WITHOUT EPISIOTOMY:

* Your partner will want to gently wash herself with warm water and refrain from using abrasive sponges, loofahs, and similar other bathing tools. If she would like to use soap, suggest that she avoid using antibacterial soap, which can be harsh. A sensitive body part benefits from a pure cleansing product made without artificial colors and fragrance. Consider presenting her with a beautifully wrapped bar of glycerin soap as a welcome-home gift. You can purchase glycerin soap at your local health food store.

* Many hospitals also provide new mothers with plastic squirt bottles for filling with warm water to assist them in keeping the vaginal area clean. Your partner will want to be gentle with these bottles to avoid irritating this sensitive area.

* In addition, consider bringing home unscented and uncolored toilet paper.

* If your partner is in the habit of douching, suggest that she forgo this aspect of her bathing routine for the first six weeks after delivery.

* Sleeping on clean sheets can assist in healing. While your partner is healing, change her sheets frequently and launder them with a mild detergent specifically designed for sensitive skin.

AFTER C-SECTION:

* Apart from cleaning and caring for the C-section incision as directed by your partner's physician, your partner should not touch the area around her C-section scar until after the bandages and sutures have been removed or dissolved and she has been given permission to bathe normally by her physician.

* Your partner will want to gently wash the rest of her body with warm water and refrain from using abrasive sponges, loofahs, and similar other bathing tools. If she would like to use soap, suggest that she avoid using antibacterial soap, which can be harsh. A sensitive body part benefits from a pure cleansing product made without artificial colors and fragrance. Consider presenting her with a beautifully wrapped bar of glycerin soap as a welcome-home gift. You can purchase glycerin soap at your local health food store.

* Sleeping on clean sheets can assist in healing. While your partner is healing, change her sheets frequently and launder them with a mild detergent specifically designed for sensitive skin.

When to Get More Help:

If your partner still experiences discomfort when she washes or handles her vaginal area more than two weeks after the birth, or if her discomfort seems to be getting worse suggest that she contact her physician to rule out infection.

2
RECOVERY AFTER C-SECTION

Caring for C-Section Wounds

The Facts:

Care of new mothers who have given birth by C-section needn't be drastically different from that given to women who have delivered vaginally. Nevertheless, in many hospitals mothers who are recovering from C-section are treated as invalids, with heavy restrictions placed on food and activity. Happily, in a growing number of hospitals this is no longer the case. New mothers are given food and encouraged to leave their beds within the first six to ten hours after delivery, since early activity is now recognized as a key to quick physical recovery.

However, a C-section is a major surgical procedure that comes with the following risks:

⊙ pain

⊙ scar infection

⊙ bladder infection

⊙ chemical dependence

For more information on the new mother's needs as she recovers from childbirth, whether by C-section or vaginal delivery, see "A New Mother's General State after Delivery" (page 22).

What You Can Do:

PAIN:
It's best when mothers recovering from C-section are *not* "knocked out" by the medication they receive after delivery, including medication given to them while they are in the hospital. Why? Heavy sedatives contain narcotics and tend to

⊙ decrease mobility, thereby slowing down healing

⊙ increase constipation and the chance of developing hemorrhoids

- produce hallucinations that prevent the woman from functioning effectively

Instead of prescribing narcotic medications, many doctors are now prescribing anti-inflammatory medications, such as prescription-strength ibuprofen. When taken by injection or orally every eight hours in the hospital, these medications have been shown to prevent pain just as effectively as narcotic medications in the majority of patients, *without* the unpleasant side effects of narcotics.

* Once a new mother returns home, she may continue to manage her pain with anti-inflammatory medications in pill form, with approval from her physician, taking 200 to 800 milligrams three times daily with food. Help your partner by keeping track of her medication schedule, keeping her supply of pain medications stocked, and bringing her water whenever she needs to take a pill.

! New mothers who use any pain medications with acetaminophen, such as Tylenol, Tylenol with Codeine, Tylenol 3, and Tylenol 4, should be aware that these medications can be very hard on the liver. To assist her liver in processing acetaminophen, the new mother can take 250 milligrams of N-acetylcysteine (NAC) at the time the acetaminophen pill is taken.

SCAR INFECTION:
A C-section scar, like any other surgical scar, is vulnerable to infection. Signs of infection include redness, swelling, heat, and increased pain in the immediate area of the incision. Follow the recommendations below to prevent infection.

* Keep the scar area clean and uncovered. Only cover the scar with a bandage if it produces a constant discharge.

* Visit your local health food store or pharmacy and purchase arnica in sublingual (under the tongue) form. Arnica is a

homeopathic remedy that helps prevent infection and promotes healing. In the first week, your partner may take it every
few hours that she is awake, and after that, three to four
times per day when awake until six weeks postpartum. Use as
directed. Arnica is safe for use when breastfeeding. Signs of
too much arnica in the system are vomiting, weakness,
increased heart rate, and nervous disturbances.

* Also look for bromelain, a digestive enzyme that also functions
  as an anti-inflammatory and healing aid. Your partner may
  take the recommended dosage three times daily for two weeks
  following delivery. Bromelain should be taken on an empty
  stomach and is safe for use when breastfeeding.

* The new mother will also greatly benefit from a liver cleansing
  formula that includes N-acetylcysteine (NAC), milk thistle,
  methionine, and inositol. Look for liver cleansing formulas at
  your local health food store or pharmacy; your partner should
  use them as directed and take them with food. Too much may
  cause loose bowels. Over-the-counter liver cleansing formulas
  are safe for use when breastfeeding.

BLADDER INFECTION:
Bladder infections can occur after C-section as a result of the
catheter used during and after delivery and as a result of urinary
retention caused by the epidural.

* To prevent bladder infection, new mothers should make a
  point of staying well hydrated by drinking at least twelve
  glasses of water daily for the first two weeks after delivery.
  Place a pitcher of water at your partner's bedside and keep it
  filled with fresh water while she is recovering.

* Visit your local health food store for pure, unsweetened cranberry juice sold in the *freshly squeezed* refrigerated section.
  Pure cranberry juice is an easy, natural aid to helping the body
  combat urinary tract infections.

CHEMICAL DEPENDENCE:

New mothers who are given narcotic pain medications such as Percocet, Darvocet, and codeine should be aware of the risk of becoming addicted to them. These pain medications should be used sparingly—ideally only at night—with decreasing frequency during the first few weeks after delivery.

* Help your partner avoid becoming dependent on her pain medication by keeping track of her medication schedule. For more information, see "Use of Pain Medication While Caring for an Infant & Breastfeeding Following Delivery" (page 60).

When to Get More Help:

PAIN:

Consult your partner's physician if she:

- ⊙ continues to feel pain or experiences an increase in pain, despite taking medication as directed

- ⊙ doesn't decrease her use of pain medication after the first two weeks following C-section

SCAR INFECTION:

Call your partner's physician if she develops a fever, if the scar opens and secretes fluid, or if her pain increases.

BLADDER INFECTION:

Call your partner's physician if your partner experiences more frequent or painful urination or notices blood in her urine within forty-eight hours to one week after delivery.

CHEMICAL DEPENDENCE:

Call your partner's physician if her use of pain medication increases rather than tapers off in the weeks following delivery.

Exercise & Activity after C-Section

The Facts:

Historically, new mothers who delivered by C-section were instructed to be "out of commission" for the first six weeks of their baby's life. Even absent a doctor's recommendation, some C-section mothers choose to spend a few weeks in bed and remain relatively inactive. Today, however, more and more physicians are recognizing that early activity after C-section—often within the first six to twelve hours—aids in quicker, less complicated healing and helps to prevent constipation and hemorrhoids.

In general, there is no medical reason for new mothers to avoid gentle physical activity—even abdominal exercise and ascending and descending stairs—unless the C-section involved the severing of the abdominal muscles, which is extremely rare. Of course, every mother should listen to her body, never over-exerting herself if she feels pain. Allow your partner to determine when she is ready to resume activity and physical exercise—don't push her.

? Why do some mothers avoid mobility after C-section? Due to the pain associated with movement after C-section, some new mothers make every effort to avoid moving. When they start moving around, though, they find that the discomfort associated with initial movement quickly fades. Overall, mobility helps to decrease pain!

What You Can Do:

* While your partner is still in the hospital, talk with her physician and nurses about helping her become mobile as soon as she can get up without feeling dizzy or falling.

* At home, encourage your partner to be as active as possible, subject to the approval of her physician. Initially, her activity may be limited to simple movements such as walking from one room to another. In general, for the first six weeks after C-section, a new mother should refrain from engaging in exercise that was prohibited during her pregnancy. After six weeks, a new mother's activity need not be restricted.

* New mothers benefit when they schedule their pain medication in a manner that allows for activity. For example, if a new mother takes her pain medication at 11:00 A.M. and 3:00 P.M., she might plan to be out of bed from 11:30 A.M. to 1:00 P.M. and then rest again until it's time for her next scheduled dose of medication at 3:00 P.M. Help your partner develop a pain medication schedule that works for her.

* Encourage your partner to discuss her plans for exercise with her physician when she goes in for her post-delivery checkup. Suggest that she also ask her physician to describe the types of discomfort that would require her to call for an evaluation.

* Once she feels more comfortable, a new mother may step up her activity by taking faster, more energetic walks. In some cases, an increase in frequency and length of activity may lead to a temporary increase in pain. This pain is a signal that the new mother has done too much, too soon. Simply scaling down the activity a bit for a few days should alleviate any temporary pain.

- If a new mother participates in yoga, Pilates, or other activity that involves stretching, remind her to refrain from stretches or positions that cause discomfort.

- If a new mother's exercise program includes weight training, bicycle riding, or any activity that requires maintaining balance, encourage her to avoid resuming these activities until she feels fully confident in her ability to balance.

When to Get More Help:

Suggest that your partner call her physician if her pain increases rather than decreases with time.

Diet after C-Section

The Facts:

In the past, new mothers in North America who gave birth by C-section were not given food for several days. Today, the majority of North American physicians no longer insist on starving mothers who are recovering from C-section, although in unusual cases solid food may be withheld if the new mother experiences trapped gas, a significant swelling of the abdomen, or an absence of bowel movements in the first few days following C-section.

What You Can Do:

* New mothers should return to a normal, healthy diet as soon as possible. Help your partner by preparing (or bringing home) nutritious, satisfying meals while she is recovering. Make sure your kitchen is stocked with plenty of healthy, easy-to-eat foods. For information on how new mothers (including those who are breastfeeding) may plan meals to promote a return to pre-pregnancy weight, see "Ideal Postpartum Diet" (page 148).

When to Get More Help:

Call your partner's physician if she experiences severe nausea, pain, gas, or vomiting during the first six weeks after C-section.

Constipation & Gas Pain after C-Section

The Facts:

Any surgery that involves opening the abdominal cavity may result in gas pain and decreased bowel movement. A new mother who is experiencing this problem is likely to feel pain on the right side of her abdomen, just under the liver, in the first few days after the surgery. It is very rare for women to suffer from this discomfort once they have been discharged from the hospital.

What You Can Do:

* Encourage your partner to get out of bed as soon as she feels comfortable, with the approval of her physician. Early mobility will promote movement of the bowels and encourage faster healing after her surgery.

* The hospital staff are likely to give the new mother a water enema. This will help flush out excess gas. Respect her desire for privacy if she requests that you leave the room during this procedure. Alternatively, if she so wishes, hold her hand while she undergoes this uncomfortable procedure.

* If her physician gives his or her approval, encourage your partner to take mineral oil by mouth, approximately 1 to 2 teaspoons once daily for no more than two days in a row. This oil will not be absorbed by the body but will rather travel through the digestive system, moving air out with it. Mineral oil is safe for use when breastfeeding.

* Encourage your partner to prevent or treat constipation by following the recommendations outlined in "Constipation" (page 160).

When to Get More Help:

Contact your partner's physician if she experiences gas pain or bloating that increases or that is accompanied by pain, nausea, and vomiting.

Scheduled C-Section

The Facts:

If you, your partner, and her physician have decided to schedule an elective C-section, there are several steps you can take to help your partner recover as quickly as possible.

What You Can Do:

* Visit your local health food store or pharmacy for arnica tablets, a homeopathic sublingual (under the tongue) supplement that helps reduce bruising, prevents infection, and promotes healing. Encourage your partner to take the directed dosage three times daily for two days prior to her C-section, including the night before and the morning of the procedure. Because arnica is not absorbed through the gastrointestinal system, your partner can take it and still comply with the requirement that she not eat prior to surgery. Use as directed. Arnica is safe for use when breastfeeding. Signs of too much arnica in the system are vomiting, weakness, increased heart rate, and nervous disturbances.

* Visit your local health food store for a liver cleansing formula that will help process the medications and other complex substances that burden the liver during and after surgery. As a result, the body will heal more quickly. Encourage your partner to take this formula twice daily with her meals, beginning one week prior to the C-section. She should reduce her intake if she experiences a loose stool.

When to Get More Help:

Encourage your partner to inform her physician if she intends to take arnica, a liver cleanser, or any other supplements.

3 PAIN MANAGEMENT

Use of Pain Medication While Caring for an Infant & Breastfeeding Following Delivery

The Facts:

Most new mothers end up using *some* sort of pain relief medication while in the hospital, whether they deliver vaginally or by C-section. Many women also need medication for pain relief after they return home with the baby, especially during the first few days. So what pain management aid is best?

In years past, many doctors routinely prescribed narcotics to new mothers for pain relief. Ideally, however, new mothers should avoid narcotics, because of the following reasons:

- ⊙ **Narcotics are strong sedatives.** New mothers who take larger doses of narcotics can expect to spend the first weeks of their baby's life in a sedated state, possibly unable to lift or care for their newborn independently.

- ⊙ **Narcotics inhibit activity.** New mothers who use narcotics take longer to become active after the delivery, which slows down their rate of recovery.

- ⊙ **Narcotics can adversely affect mood.** New mothers often find that their moods vary widely depending on when they took their last dose. For example, in the hour or so prior to her next scheduled dose of pain medication, a new mother may feel anxious and moody.

- ⊙ **Narcotics adversely affect bowel function.** One common side effect of narcotics is increased constipation, which may aggravate rectal or rectal muscle tears.

- ⊙ **Narcotics are addictive.** Many new mothers struggle to wean themselves from these powerful medications.

In light of these negative effects, doctors have begun recommending stronger versions of aspirin, acetaminophen (commonly marketed as Tylenol), and ibuprofen in place of narcotics. Today, many women receive these medications in pill form or by injection (in a stronger dosage) while in the hospital. The results have been remarkable. Women enjoy pain relief without the negative side effects of narcotics, which allows them to be more active immediately after their delivery, speeding up their recovery, and thereby causing them to require less pain medication once they get home. More than half of the women who use ibuprofen never need anything stronger. Those who require stronger medications generally need them only at night.

One bit of good news is this: when a new mother takes anti-inflammatory medications or mild narcotics, she may still breastfeed without negatively affecting her baby. In fact, only traces of codeine, acetaminophen, and ibuprofen have been shown to filter down into the breast milk, with no negative effects on the baby.*

What You Can Do:

A new mother who enjoyed a relatively smooth delivery that did not result in a tear or an episiotomy will usually require little or no pain medication for delivery-related pain. However, your partner may still need a mild pain reliever to manage the discomfort associated with postpartum cramping of the uterus. See "Postpartum Cramping" (page 28) for more information. The use of pain medication is more common among new mothers who sustained cuts or tears while giving birth.

* If your partner chooses to avoid narcotics, make sure she leaves the hospital with a prescription for ibuprofen. She may take up to 800 milligrams every eight hours with the approval of her physician.

---

* One unusual report indicated that an infant developed a rash when his mother consumed acetaminophen.

* If her physician recommends acetaminophen, commonly marketed as Tylenol, she should use it as instructed, but she may want to keep in mind that this medication can be hard on her liver. Suggest that she add the supplement N-acetylcysteine (NAC) along with the acetaminophen dosage, to remedy this problem. You can find this supplement at your local health food store. She can take 250 milligrams NAC each time the acetaminophen pill is taken.

* A few new mothers will require stronger pain medication. Taking small quantities of narcotic pain medication increases their ability to heal, breathe, and get moving again. After all, some of us just happen to be more sensitive to pain than others. If your partner finds that she requires stronger medication, act as her advocate. Call her physician and help her obtain a prescription for one of several strong pain relievers that contain relatively mild narcotics, including Vicodin, Tylenol with Codeine, Darvocet, or Percocet, but be aware (and make sure she's aware) that these drugs can be addictive. Medications of this type should not be taken casually. Ideally, your partner should take acetaminophen or ibuprofen during the day and occasionally add a stronger medication at bedtime, when needed. She may continue this treatment for no more than two weeks.

When to Get More Help:

If your partner did not sustain any tears or episiotomy cuts during childbirth but indicates that she is experiencing a significant increase of her uterine cramping, suggest that she contact her physician to rule out uterine infection.

If your partner sustained a vaginal tear or underwent an episiotomy, her need for pain medication should gradually become less intense during the first few weeks. If this is not the case, seek a medical evaluation to rule out infection in her tear or episiotomy site.

If the delivery was a C-section and your partner indicates that her pain is restricting her ability to move—so much so that she cannot breathe deeply without experiencing pain or can't get out of bed—be her advocate and make sure that her physician rules out infection and otherwise provides her with proper pain relief to enable her to function.

In extremely rare cases, a new mother who continues to ask for pain medication may not have a problem with pain but may instead be developing an addiction to her narcotic pain medication. In such a case, her pain medication requests may increase rather than decrease over several weeks. If you believe that your partner is becoming dependent on her pain medication, don't judge her. Instead, help her by contacting her physician for a referral to a pain specialist who can help her free herself from pain medications.

Back Pain

The Facts:

A new mother may experience back pain after delivery, even if she has never suffered from back discomfort during or prior to pregnancy, due to the following factors:

- The spine may have been subjected to unusual pressure or twisted in an unnatural way during labor, due to the numbness caused by the epidural.

- Even without epidural, a prolonged "pushing" stage of labor may have put pressure on pelvic nerves, which causes symptoms similar to back and pelvic pain.

- The coccyx, or tail bone, may have been bruised or fractured during labor.

- If the pregnancy included a long period of bed rest or relative inactivity, the mother's muscles may have become weak and therefore more susceptible to injury during a strenuous labor.

- The site of the epidural may be tender and uncomfortable.

What You Can Do:

PREVENTION:

⁕ Unless she is otherwise advised by her physician, encourage your partner to remain active throughout her pregnancy. This will ensure that her back is strong enough to withstand the rigors of labor. Pre-pregnancy abdominal workouts can be maintained until the fourteenth week. From the fifteenth week on, gentler abdominal workouts are recommended. Swimming is an excellent low-impact back-strengthening exercise throughout pregnancy. Encourage your partner to ask her physician what back-strengthening exercises he or she recommends.

* Sleeping with strategically positioned pillows during pregnancy can help to prevent back strain. Throughout her pregnancy, encourage her to sleep on her side, with one pillow under her neck and a second pillow between her legs. (Lying flat on her back may cut off blood flow to the baby.)

! Pregnant women should not use back–support belts designed for weight lifters and moving professionals, because these belts put pressure on the abdomen. Help your partner find one of several back straps designed for pregnant women that lift the abdomen, giving support to the back and the uterus. She should wear this strap loosely around her abdomen.

* If your partner experiences minimal or intermittent back pain, visit your pharmacy for mild, over-the-counter anti-inflammatory medications, such as ibuprofen; a heating pad; and menthol-based heat creams especially formulated for muscle pain. Ask the pharmacist for additional recommendations.

* For a new mother who prefers natural remedies to treat her back pain, visit your local health food store for herbal heat patches and natural anti-inflammatory aids.

* Additionally, many new mothers find that acupuncture and chiropractic treatments are helpful in reducing back pain. Assist her in seeking out pain specialists, including those physicians trained in Prolo Therapy, a breastfeeding-safe treatment wherein a pain trigger point is injected with local

anesthesia and concentrated sugar. This therapy is designed to relieve pain and the inflammation that causes it.

When to Get More Help:

If your partner experiences ongoing pain or if she feels increasing pain in the area where her epidural was administered (i.e., in the small of her back), immediately contact her physician for an examination. See "Pain & Redness at the Epidural Site" (page 67) for more information.

Pain & Redness at the Epidural Site

The Facts:

In extremely rare situations, the site of the epidural becomes infected; this infection may spread to the spinal cord. The main symptom of this condition is severe pain in the epidural site that increases rapidly with every passing day. The area will become red and extremely tender. An infection of the epidural site must be treated immediately with antibiotic medication. Failure to receive this treatment can be severely detrimental to a woman's health.

What You Can Do:

An infection of the epidural site must be treated right away. If you think your partner's epidural site is infected, call her physician and alert him or her. This condition always requires immediate treatment in the hospital in order to avoid tragic consequences.

Because your partner will be hospitalized and you'll need to be at her side, arrange for a trusted family member to care for the baby while you help your partner in the hospital.

When to Get More Help:

Call your partner's physician immediately if you suspect that your partner's epidural site may be infected. Expect to bring your partner to the hospital for an aggressive course of treatment with antibiotic medication.

Carpal Tunnel Syndrome

The Facts:

Surprisingly, carpal tunnel syndrome that is experienced immediately after delivery is directly related to the water that pregnant women begin retaining on the day following the birth of their baby. See "Water Retention: Swollen Feet, Ankles & Hands" (page 34) for more information.

What's the connection between water retention and carpal tunnel syndrome? One of the nerves that controls hand function is enveloped by a ligament at the wrist. When a new mother's body retains water, this ligament becomes swollen along with the rest of her body. The swollen ligament puts pressure on this hand-controlling nerve and creates pain, pressure, and decreased mobility in the fingers.

What You Can Do:

Helping your partner avoid water retention will assist in reducing her carpal tunnel syndrome discomfort:

* Encourage her to supplement her diet with magnesium glycinate, magnesium gluconate, magnesium citrate, magnesium aspartate, or other fast-absorbing magnesium available from your local health food store. She should take the suggested dosage with food and slowly increase her intake every few days until her swelling and pain decrease. She should reduce her dosage if she experiences fatigue, muscle weakness, or diarrhea and taper off dosage when swelling and pain cease.

* If your partner is taking magnesium, she might consider adding vitamin B complex to her supplement program. A dosage of 25 to 50 milligrams per day will increase the efficiency of her magnesium supplement and will also boost her energy. She might also try 100 milligrams of vitamin B_6 twice daily.

- Evening primrose oil capsules with the active ingredient gamma linolenic acid, also available in your health food store, can help reduce your partner's swelling. A dose containing 125 milligrams of gamma linolenic acid should be taken with breakfast. Evening primrose oil is safe for use when breastfeeding.

- Make your partner a salad or smoothie that includes parsley, cilantro, dill, cucumber, green pepper, asparagus, watermelon, or dandelion greens. All of these are natural diuretics and are helpful in reducing water retention.

- Encourage your partner to lie down and relax. Lying in a horizontal position promotes the reabsorption of the retained water. Of course, she won't take this advice unless you're caring for the baby while she's taking a break. Offer to watch the baby, so that she feels comfortable taking a moment for herself.

- Draw a warm bath for your partner. Take care of the baby or arrange for someone else to do so while she soaks. Immersing her entire body in the water will help move fluid away from her extremities while giving her a much-deserved break from the overwhelming job of motherhood.

- Unless otherwise indicated by her physician, a woman does not need to restrict salt consumption simply because she is retaining water. Sodium should be restricted only when water retention increases immediately after she eats salty food.

- Many new mothers who wish to avoid pain medication find acupuncture to be helpful in alleviating carpal tunnel syndrome pain. Also see the "Use of Pain Medication" section (page 60) for more information.

* Bracing the wrist can also be helpful. You or your partner might want to ask your pharmacist or an orthopedic surgeon to provide her with a removable wrist brace.

When to Get More Help:

Consult your partner's physician for a referral when your partner's wrist pain is so great that she cannot perform her daily tasks.

4 SLEEP & ENERGY ADJUSTMENT

Fatigue & Exhaustion

The Facts:

Have you ever met a new mother in the first few months of her child's life who reports that she's more energetic than ever? Not many people have. Motherhood is an exhausting job. Add the tasks of recovering from pregnancy and childbirth, adjusting to an entirely new role in life, and having to do all of this with little sleep, and you've got one tired mom. But how can one differentiate "normal" new-mother fatigue and fatigue that requires help? To answer this question, you'll need to understand what causes fatigue. Below are some of the common culprits:

- sleep disruption
- sleep deprivation
- insomnia
- depression and/or anxiety
- abrupt recognition of the challenges of new motherhood
- too much to do and not enough time
- anemia, a consequence of excessive blood loss after delivery, which leads to iron deficiency
- poor nutrition
- pain associated with the delivery
- thyroid abnormality
- adrenal insufficiency, malfunction, and exhaustion
- lack of activity
- mineral deficiency
- estrogen deficiency
- melatonin deficiency

What You Can Do:

* Helping your partner get more and better sleep is perhaps the best thing you can do for her, for yourself, and for your baby. It will help her avoid exhaustion and many of the symptoms generally associated with "baby blues" and postpartum depression. For more information on what you can do to help her sleep, see "Sleep Deprivation & Insomnia" (page 76).

* If you believe that your partner is suffering from mild or serious depression or anxiety, helping her manage her emotional state will also help her manage her exhaustion. For more information, see "Mild Mood Swings" (page 81) and Part Two of this guidebook, "The New Mother's Mind: Recognizing, Preventing & Treating Postpartum Depression & Mood Changes."

* New mothers are confronted with a whole new world of baby-care responsibilities and emotional and physical challenges on the day they return from the hospital. Trying to manage even a small portion of these challenges can be overwhelming and exhausting for the new mother, who is still healing from the delivery. For tips on helping your partner juggle the many aspects of being a new mother, see Part Three of this guidebook, "The New Mother's Life: The Challenges of Balancing Baby, Self & Partner."

- Anemia, a consequence of excessive blood loss after childbirth, which leads to iron deficiency, can cause fatigue. See "Blood Loss after Delivery & Anemia" (page 41) for more information.

- If your partner fails to fuel her body with food, she cannot expect her body to heal properly, perform at optimal levels, or produce enough milk for the baby during this challenging time. For more information on proper nutrition for the new mother, see "Ideal Postpartum Diet" (page 148).

- A constant feeling of pain—even low-grade pain—can wear anyone down. Help your partner manage her postpartum pain by referring to chapter 3, "Pain Management."

- A properly functioning thyroid gland is essential for maintaining adequate energy. For information on thyroid deficiency, see "Thyroid Disorder That Develops after Delivery" (page 91).

- The adrenal gland is responsible for bursts of energy, strength, and stamina. Unfortunately, when this gland malfunctions or becomes exhausted, extreme fatigue follows. For more information on how you can help your partner determine whether her adrenal gland requires attention, see "Fatigue Due to Adrenal Gland Exhaustion" (page 95).

- The less active the new mother is after delivery, the longer it will take for her to resume her normal level of activity. Unfortunately, many women limit their own activity in the weeks following childbirth because they are afraid of aggravating their delivery wounds. For information on how your partner can resume her activity without injuring herself, see "Exercise & Activity after Vaginal Delivery" (page 153) or "Exercise & Activity after C-Section" (page 52).

- A diet containing minerals like sodium, magnesium, copper, potassium, and zinc is essential for maintaining overall good health and energy. For information on whether your partner is low on required minerals, see "Maintaining Hydration" in the chapter on breastfeeding (page 123).

* On the day after delivery, the new mother's estrogen level drops dramatically and does not rebound for several weeks or months. This deficiency may cause her to experience fatigue. For information on how you can help your partner regain her optimal estrogen level, see "Depression, Memory Loss & Insomnia Due to Estrogen Deficiency" (page 99).

* Melatonin is the body's natural sleep aid. When a new mother's body fails to produce enough melatonin, lack of sleep, fatigue, and exhaustion are likely consequences. For information on how you can help your partner get enough melatonin, see "Poor Sleep Due to Melatonin Deficiency" (page 104) and "Sleep Deprivation & Insomnia" (page 76).

* Finally, low blood sugar, or hypoglycemia, may cause a new mother to feel fatigued, even with sufficient sleep. For information on how you can help your partner identify and remedy this condition, see "Hypoglycemia, or Low Blood Sugar" (page 106).

When to Get More Help:

If your partner continues to feel fatigued despite following the recommendations outlined above—particularly if she has complied with the recommendations for sleep, diet, and anemia—encourage her to contact her physician or a nutrition-oriented doctor, who may analyze her hormone levels to see if they are the source of her fatigue.

Sleep Deprivation & Insomnia

The Facts:

Sleep deprivation and insomnia are the causes of many serious health concerns associated with new motherhood. Nearly *all* of the problems facing new mothers originate in lack of sleep, including:

- ⊙ low energy level

- ⊙ low mental focus and confusion

- ⊙ irritability

- ⊙ depression

- ⊙ diminished coordination

- ⊙ little or no interest in maintaining outward appearance

- ⊙ little or no interest in losing pregnancy weight

- ⊙ little or no sex drive

Why is it so difficult for new mothers to sleep well?

- ⊙ A new baby's initial sleeping and feeding schedule disrupts her nighttime sleep every few hours.

- ⊙ Extra adrenaline, which helps her keep up with baby-related responsibilities during the day, also keeps her up at night.

- ⊙ She is worried about the well-being of her new baby and her ability to care for him or her.

- She becomes depressed or anxious.

- Tension between family members arises due to the challenges of having a new baby in the house.

- She lacks an extended family's emotional and physical support or other sources of support.

- She feels that she must do everything herself.

- She experiences estrogen deficiency, progesterone deficiency, or melatonin deficiency.

? Can all new mothers expect to become sleep deprived? Not necessarily. Some women have the ability to fall asleep very quickly and do so after feeding their babies every few hours during the night. Some women are also lucky enough to have babies who sleep most of the night or quickly fall into a daytime sleep schedule that allows them to nap, catch up on work, exercise, and socialize. For women and babies for whom this does *not* occur naturally, the sleep-related sections in this guidebook offer sleep tips that may assist new parents.

What You Can Do:

* Prior to the birth of your baby, make a sleep strategy with your partner so you can both get enough sleep after you bring your baby home. Whether you take turns getting up to care for the baby during the night or solicit the help of a family member or outside caregiver, it is essential that both parents get time to sleep. There is no need for both parents to be awake every night. See "A Parent's Guide to Adjusting to New Sleep Patterns" in Part Three of this guidebook (page 228) for specific information on how both you and your partner can get enough sleep.

* If your partner is breastfeeding and the baby wakes her frequently to nurse, give her a night (or part of one) off. During the day, she can use a breast pump to express milk; when she

has stored up enough milk to cover the nighttime feedings, you can give the baby the stored milk in a bottle while she sleeps.

* It is common for new mothers and fathers who have been given the night off to be woken up by the cry of their newborn or by a light switched on by the on-duty parent. Help your partner get the full benefit of her night off by suggesting that she use inexpensive earplugs and a sleep mask when she is off duty. If necessary, the off-duty parent can sleep in a separate room.

* Help the new mother arrange for a family member, friend, or hired caregiver to watch the baby for a few hours during the day while she naps.

* Encourage your partner to be calm throughout the day. Running around in a panic will affect her ability to get to sleep—even hours later. Suggest that she meditate, stretch, or take a warm bath while the baby naps. Many baby beds can be carried into the bathroom if there is no one available to watch the baby while she bathes.

* Many new mothers hesitate to use natural sleeping aids because they fear that the medications will prevent them from waking in response to their baby's cry. However, new mothers are programmed to be sensitive to the high-pitched cry of their baby, and babies are programmed to cry louder and louder until their mother responds. And medical studies have yet to show that a baby who cries out for his mother a minute or two longer than usual while her mother awakens is damaged in the slightest.

* Both new mothers and fathers may also choose from a variety of supplements, including fast-absorbing magnesium, to help them relax and sleep. Visit your local health food store for fast-absorbing magnesium, such as magnesium glycinate, magnesium gluconate, magnesium citrate, or magnesium

aspartate in capsules or sublingual (under the tongue) drops. A new mother might consider taking 200 to 300 milligrams in pill or sublingual-drop form just before bedtime. She should reduce her dosage if she feels fatigued, if her muscles feel weak, or if she experiences diarrhea. If your partner believes that she may be using too much magnesium, she can visit her physician for a blood test to evaluate the level of magnesium in her red blood cells. *If your partner has a history of kidney function problems, she should use magnesium only under the strict supervision of a physician.* Magnesium is safe for use when breastfeeding.

* Tryptophan is a natural substance found in milk and turkey that promotes sleep. You may obtain this amino acid in supplement form at your local health food store. A new mother may take 500 to 1500 milligrams one-half hour before bedtime. Tryptophan is safe for use when breastfeeding.

* Both new parents can help themselves get to sleep and stay asleep by supplementing their diet with melatonin, a hormone that is essential for proper sleep. Melatonin supplements in capsule and sublingual drops are available at your local pharmacy or health food store. You and your partner should choose a form of melatonin that is synthetically produced, not extracted from animals. Begin with 1 milligram and increase your dosage daily by 1 milligram, but take no more than 7 milligrams daily. Most men and women will not tolerate more than 3 milligrams. You and your partner should reduce the dosage if you find that you rise too early, experience disturbing dreams, or wake up feeling groggy. When using melatonin during the day in order to help you nap, use an eye mask to block out daylight. Melatonin is safe for use when breastfeeding.

* Many new mothers—feeling thrilled, scared, and overwhelmed by the responsibility of raising a tiny baby to adulthood—find that their worries about their baby prevent them from sleeping. If your partner falls into this category, be as understanding

and supportive as possible—you are fortunate that the mother of your child is so committed to protecting his or her well-being. Listen to her concerns and do what you can to make sure your baby is healthy and safe. Reassure her that her body and her natural maternal instincts have prepared her for her new role. Suggest that she consult your baby's pediatrician and speak to women in her family or circle of friends regarding how they have dealt with similar issues. Assist her by speaking to colleagues, visiting your local bookstore, or consulting on-line resources for information on her specific concerns. If you feel that your partner's fears are disproportionate to the reality of your baby's situation, see chapters 7 and 8 on postpartum depression for more information.

When to Get More Help:

If your partner implements the above recommendations but still has trouble sleeping, encourage her to ask her physician about a prescription for natural progesterone. Both new mothers and new fathers who have trouble sleeping may benefit from using natural progesterone as a sleeping aid. New mothers may take 50 to 150 milligrams in pill form or in sublingual (under the tongue) drop form one-half hour before bedtime. New fathers may take 50 to 150 milligrams in pill form one-half hour before bedtime. New mothers who wake to breastfeed after only a few hours of sleep should begin with a lower dose, since progesterone often makes men and women dizzy. Progesterone is safe for use when breastfeeding.

Alternatively, because her sleep is so critical to her health and to your family, suggest that she speak to her physician about a short-term prescription for sleeping aids.

Mild Mood Swings, Including Mild Anxiety & Depression

The Facts:

Virtually every new mother experiences some emotional ups and downs in the first few weeks and months after giving birth. Mild depression and anxiety related to the physical and emotional changes and challenges of new motherhood are common. If you believe your partner's depression and anxiety are more serious, see Part Two of this guidebook, "The New Mother's Mind: Recognizing, Preventing & Treating Postpartum Depression & Mood Changes."

What You Can Do:

MILD ANXIETY:

* Encourage your partner to get as much sleep as possible. Sleep deprivation is a common cause of anxiety in new mothers. Help your partner get the sleep she needs by offering to watch the baby or arranging for a family member or professional to watch the baby so that she can sleep late in the morning, sleep through the night, or nap during the day. See "Sleep Deprivation & Insomnia" (page 76) and "A Parent's Guide to Adjusting to New Sleep Patterns" (page 228) for more information.

* Dehydration is another common cause of anxiety and irritability. Remind your partner to drink enough mineral-rich water, and bring her a glass of water whenever she is nursing the baby. A new mother should drink eight to twelve glasses of water daily—and more if she is breastfeeding.

? What is "mineral-rich" water? In its most natural state, water contains sodium, magnesium, iron, potassium, and copper—minerals essential for maintaining proper body functions. Although spring and artesian waters can supply our bodies with many of these minerals, filtered water may have had these elements removed. The next time you purchase bottled water, inspect the nutritional information chart on the label—do you see a column of zeros? If so, the water you've purchased does not contain the minerals your body requires. To ensure that you, your partner, and your baby ingest these beneficial elements, create a natural electrolyte-rich sports drink by adding sea salt and honey to your water. Start by adding small amounts of sea salt and honey and increase both to suit your partner's taste.

* Your partner is likely to feel anxious if she does not eat enough nutritious food, especially while her body is healing from child-birth and adjusting to its post-pregnant state. Encourage her to eat three meals and two snacks daily that provide her with enough proteins and fats to sustain her during this challenging time. Help out by doing the grocery shopping and purchasing healthy, easy-to-prepare foods. Ease her burden by getting involved in meal preparation whenever you can. See "Ideal Postpartum Diet" (page 148) for more information.

* Inactivity is a major cause of anxiety in new mothers—especially women who enjoyed an active social and professional life prior to the birth of their baby. Help your partner resume her normal activity and social schedule as soon as she feels well enough by watching the baby or arranging for a family member or professional caregiver to watch the baby.

* Taking a natural form of the hormone progesterone in sublingual (under the tongue) drops or capsules can help reduce anxiety. See "Postpartum Depression (Dominated by Anxiety & Panic)" (page 194) for more information on how to use this supplement. Your partner should use one-quarter of the dosage recommended for postpartum depression as a starting dose. Natural progesterone is available by prescription from "compounding" pharmacies, pharmacies that formulate medications on a special-order basis and often specialize in

formulating natural hormones. Progesterone is safe for use when breastfeeding.

* Magnesium supplements are incredibly effective for calming anxiety. Visit your local health food store for fast-absorbing magnesium, such as magnesium glycinate, magnesium gluconate, magnesium citrate, or magnesium aspartate, in capsules or sublingual (under the tongue) drops. Encourage your partner to take the dosage suggested on the bottle and slowly increase the dosage every few days. She should reduce her dosage if she feels fatigued, if her muscles feel weak, or if she experiences diarrhea. If your partner believes that she may be using too much magnesium, she can visit her physician for a blood test to evaluate the level of magnesium in her red blood cells. *If your partner has a history of kidney function problems, she should use magnesium only under the strict supervision of a physician.* Magnesium is safe for use when breastfeeding.

* Calcium depletes the body's supply of magnesium, which helps combat anxiety. If your partner is feeling anxious, suggest that she temporarily stop taking calcium supplements, including antacids and calcium-enriched foods such as orange juice.

* To help your partner reduce her anxiety, visit your local health food store for gamma-aminobutyric acid (GABA), a natural supplement that calms by stimulating the GABA receptor in the brain. Note, however, that some women do not respond to this supplement and a very small number actually experience the opposite effect—they become a bit edgy for a few hours. GABA is safe for use when breastfeeding.

* Also visit your health food store for L-theanine, a supplement that relaxes and prevents agitation, and homeopathic remedies that help reduce anxiety naturally. Suggest that she use these products as directed anytime she feels anxious. L-theanine and homeopathic remedies are safe for use when breastfeeding.

* If your partner feels panicky at night, visit your local health food store or pharmacy for melatonin. Melatonin is a natural supplement that helps bring down high adrenaline levels. Your partner can take 1 milligram one-half hour before bedtime. This dosage may be increased daily by 1 milligram but should not exceed 7 milligrams. Most people will not tolerate more than 3 milligrams. Your partner should reduce the dosage if she finds that she rises too early, experiences disturbing dreams, or wakes up feeling groggy.

* Sleep deprivation can start and exacerbate the cycle of depression. Encourage your partner to get as much sleep as she needs, and help her do this by watching the baby or having a trusted person care for the baby while she sleeps. See "A Parent's Guide to Adjusting to New Sleep Patterns" (page 228) for more information.

* Dehydration can increase feelings of depression. Remind your partner to drink enough mineral-rich water, and bring her a glass of water whenever she is nursing the baby. A new mother should drink eight to twelve glasses of water daily—and more if she is breastfeeding.

* Improper nutrition is also a common contributing factor of depression. Ensure that your partner is eating properly. Help out by doing the grocery shopping and purchasing healthy, easy-to-prepare foods. Ease her burden by getting involved in meal preparation whenever you can. See "Ideal Postpartum Diet" (page 148) for more information.

* Depression is exacerbated by inactivity and isolation. Encourage your partner to get out of the house, get some fresh air and exercise, and see and speak to people. Help her do this by watching the baby or having a trusted person care for the baby while she gets out of the house. Ask her to go for after-dinner walks around the neighborhood with you and the baby, or pack

a simple picnic and take your partner and baby to a nearby park on a sunny weekend afternoon.

* 5-hydroxytryptophan is a natural amino acid that elevates mood by turning into a substance called serotonin. You can purchase this supplement at your local health food store and suggest that your partner take 50 milligrams at both breakfast and lunch, and 50 to 150 milligrams with dinner. Suggest that she add another 50 milligrams at each meal if she doesn't feel a change within two weeks. She should reduce her dosage if she feels sleepy or has diarrhea. This remedy is not appropriate for new mothers who use an antidepressant medication in the SSRI category, such as Zoloft, Prozac, and Selexa. 5-hydroytryptophan is safe for use when breastfeeding.

* St. John's wort is another natural supplement that helps to elevate mood. Visit your local health food store for St. John's wort in .3 percent extract form. Suggest that your partner take 300 milliliters three times daily. This remedy is not appropriate for new mothers who use an antidepressant medication in the SSRI category, such as Zoloft, Prozac, and Selexa. St. John's wort is safe for use when breastfeeding.

* North Americans often worry about their cholesterol levels being too high. However, a cholesterol level that is too low can also be problematic and may be a contributing factor of mild depression. If your partner seems mildly depressed, encourage your partner to visit her physician for a cholesterol check. If her level is under 160, visit your local health food store for an amino acid supplement called inositol. Encourage her to take 8000 milligrams. Inositol is safe for use when breastfeeding.

* Your partner probably took folic acid (or prenatal vitamins containing folic acid) during her pregnancy to prevent certain birth defects, but did you know that folic acid can also help prevent depression? Folic acid may be purchased at your local

health food store or pharmacy. Suggest that she take 5 to 10 milligrams daily with a meal. Note that mothers who breastfeed and continue taking prenatal vitamins that include folic acid will still benefit from taking additional folic acid to assist with depression.

* Dopamine is an important neurotransmitter that elevates mood. Nicotinamide adenine dinucleotide (NADH) promotes the production of dopamine and is available at your local health food store. Encourage your partner to take 2.5 milligrams daily on an empty stomach. She can increase her dosage every three to four days, not to exceed 10 milligrams per day. She should reduce her dosage if she feels agitated or too relaxed. NADH is safe for use when breastfeeding.

* S-adenosylmethionine (SAMe) is a natural supplement that helps to quickly alleviate a variety of depressive moods, in addition to cleaning the liver and promoting physical healing. It's a great overall supplement for the new mother and is available at your local health food store. Suggest that your partner take 200 milligrams twice daily on an empty stomach—one in the morning and another before the sun sets. She can increase the dosage every other day, not to exceed 800 milligrams twice per day. She should reduce her dosage if she feels sleepy, edgy, or fuzzy headed. SAMe is safe for use when breastfeeding.

* Many episodes of mild depressive mood changes relate to a deficiency of amino-acid-rich foods in a new mother's diet. This is common among vegetarians. If your partner is a vegetarian, encourage her to supplement her diet with an over-the-counter amino acid formula that can be easily added to a smoothie at breakfast or to a soup at lunch or dinner. Amino acid supplement formulas may be found at your local health food store. If your partner is not a vegetarian, encourage her to eat more meat. Whenever possible, while she is breastfeeding she should consume meat from animals that were "green-

grass grown" and "non-grain fed." These kinds of meat contain more nutrients and beneficial fatty acids and are high in conjugated linoleic acid (CLA), a substance that promotes weight loss. Amino acid supplement formulas are safe for use when breastfeeding.

When to Get More Help:

If you are not sure which remedy is right for your partner, consult your physician. If the remedies outlined above do not help to alleviate your partner's mild anxiety and depression or if her symptoms worsen, see Part Two of this guidebook, "The New Mother's Mind: Recognizing, Preventing & Treating Postpartum Depression & Mood Changes," for more aggressive remedies and consult her physician.

Preexisting Thyroid Disorder

The Facts:

The thyroid gland produces a hormone crucial for optimal physical performance, including blood circulation, temperature regulation, energy level, and other important functions. New mothers who experience thyroid deficiency fall into two categories: women who have a preexisting thyroid disorder and take medication for their condition, and women who develop a thyroid deficiency during their pregnancy or after the birth of their baby. This section addresses issues affecting new mothers with a preexisting low thyroid disorder. For these women, while they may have been instructed to maintain or increase their medication during their pregnancy, it is often necessary to reduce the dosage of their thyroid medication after delivery.

? Why does the new mother need to reduce her thyroid medication dosage after she gives birth? During pregnancy, the body produces more of a protein called sex-binding globulin, which attaches itself to the thyroid hormone, requiring pregnant women to elevate the amount of thyroid medication they take. In the first six weeks after delivery, a woman's body begins producing less sex-binding globulin, requiring her to reduce her intake of thyroid medication in order to avoid symptoms that develop when the body has too much thyroid, including:

- agitation
- fast heartbeat
- inability to sleep
- excessive perspiration
- shakiness (hand tremors)

What You Can Do:

* If your partner is taking thyroid medication and experiences any of these symptoms, encourage her to lower her thyroid dosage under the supervision of her physician. Ideally, her physician will create a plan to gradually reduce her dosage, thereby avoiding a sudden drop of thyroid in her body, which would lead to unpleasant symptoms associated with thyroid deficiency.

* While your partner is reducing her dosage of thyroid medication it may drop to a level that is too low. If so, she must adjust her dosage with her physician's guidance. Symptoms of a thyroid level that is too low include

  ⊙ cold hands and feet

  ⊙ little perspiration

  ⊙ fatigue

  ⊙ headache

  ⊙ leg cramps

  ⊙ inability to "get going" in the morning

  ⊙ dry skin

  ⊙ brittle nails

  ⊙ bags under the eyes

  ⊙ hair loss

  ⊙ easy weight gain, difficult weight loss

  ⊙ constipation

  ⊙ yellow or slightly orange skin when she eats large quantities of carrots

* As your partner goes through the process of adjusting her thyroid medication, be aware of her moods. Check in with her about her symptoms in order to help her determine whether her thyroid level may be too low or high. Often, hearing the opinion of her partner or another respected person can be invaluable to a new mother, who has many new responsibilities and little time to devote to her own physical and medical needs.

When to Get More Help:

Monitoring your partner's thyroid levels requires the assistance of a physician. Encourage her to take the time to visit her doctor, have a blood test to determine her thyroid level, and create a strategy that suits her symptoms and lifestyle.

Thyroid Disorder That Develops after Delivery

The Facts:

The thyroid gland produces a hormone crucial for optimal physical performance, including blood circulation, temperature regulation, energy level, and other important functions. New mothers who experience thyroid deficiency fall into two categories: women who have a preexisting thyroid disorder and take medication for their condition, and women who develop a thyroid deficiency during their pregnancy or after the birth of their baby. This section addresses the issue of thyroid disorder that develops after delivery.

Why do women with no history of thyroid problems suddenly develop them after the birth of their baby? A common complication that occurs after delivery is a nonbacterial, or viral, infection in the thyroid gland called thyroiditis. Up to 20 percent of all new mothers experience some degree of this condition after delivery. In most cases, women will only feel a slight tenderness around the thyroid gland (located in the central lower part of the throat). With so many new sensations being felt during the weeks after delivery, it is common for this slight tenderness to be overlooked. Unfortunately, in addition to this mild symptom, the body begins to overproduce the thyroid hormone, leading to the following symptoms of thyroid overproduction:

- agitation

- fast heartbeat

- inability to sleep

- excessive perspiration

- shakiness (hand tremors)

Thyroiditis may progress from overproduction of the thyroid hormone to underproduction of the thyroid hormone, resulting in the following symptoms:

⊙ cold hands and feet

⊙ little perspiration

⊙ fatigue

⊙ headache

⊙ leg cramps

⊙ inability to "get going" in the morning

⊙ dry skin

⊙ brittle nails

⊙ bags under the eyes

⊙ hair loss

⊙ easy weight gain, difficult weight loss

⊙ constipation

⊙ yellow or slightly orange skin when she eats large quantities of carrots

! It is common for new mothers and fathers to overlook or ignore these unpleasant symptoms in the commotion associated with the arrival of a baby. However, prompt treatment of thyroiditis will greatly improve your and your partner's ability to enjoy your new parenthood.

What You Can Do:

IF YOUR PARTNER DISPLAYS THE SYMPTOMS OF THYROID OVERPRODUCTION:

✽ Encourage your partner to visit her physician and have a thyroid-stimulating hormone (TSH) test done. The TSH test is the most common method used for testing a patient's thyroid condition. Unfortunately, alone, this test often fails to demonstrate thyroid deficiency. For this reason, suggest that she ask her physician to also test her T3 Free and T4 Free levels. These tests monitor the active thyroid hormone itself. Also encourage her to ask her physician to run an antithyroid microsomal antibody test.

* If her test results indicate that her thyroid level is too high, suggest that she ask her physician for a referral to an endocrinologist, a physician specializing in hormones.

IF YOUR PARTNER DISPLAYS THE SYMPTOMS OF THYROID UNDERPRODUCTION:

* Encourage your partner to visit her physician and have a thyroid-stimulating hormone (TSH) test done. The TSH test is the most common method used for testing a patient's thyroid condition. Unfortunately, alone, this test often fails to demonstrate thyroid deficiency. For this reason, suggest that she ask her physician to also test her T3 Free and T4 Free levels. These tests monitor the active thyroid hormone itself. Also encourage her to ask her physician to run an antithyroid microsomal antibody test.

* If her T3 Free and T4 Free levels are low, or even if they are on the low end of normal, urge her to request *natural* thyroid supplements. Why should she request medication when her test indicates that her thyroid level is normal? First, she will want her body to perform at its *optimal* level during this challenging time in her life. Second, the levels considered normal may not be ideal for your partner. The range of normal is extremely wide, and as long as your partner has most of the symptoms described above, her thyroid gland is not performing optimally. Balancing her levels could dramatically improve the way she feels.

When to Get More Help:

If your partner displays the symptoms of low or high thyroid but is told that her levels are normal and that nothing can be done, seek additional information about thyroid disorder. Help your partner find a physician with experience in nutrition-oriented medicine and natural hormone replacement therapy.

Fatigue Due to Adrenal Gland Exhaustion

The Facts:

The adrenal gland produces adrenaline, noradrenaline, cortisol, DHEA, pregnenolone, and other important hormones that arm us with a survival instinct originally intended to help us flee from natural predators. Today, our bodies use the hormones produced by our adrenal gland to function effectively when we encounter or engage in stressful situations, long work hours, strenuous exercise routines, illness or allergies, and temperature and other environmental changes. While humans can live for some period of time without food or water, we could not survive for more than forty-eight hours without the hormones produced by our adrenal gland. So when this gland malfunctions or becomes exhausted, the body is dramatically affected, resulting in:

- ⊙ persistent fatigue

- ⊙ fatigue after any level of activity

- ⊙ feeling drained after an emotional exchange

- ⊙ feeling dizzy after standing up

- ⊙ intolerance to noise

- ⊙ intolerance to temperature change

- ⊙ craving of sugar, spice, or salt

- ⊙ becoming allergic to foods and environmental factors

Extreme cases of adrenal exhaustion, identified as Addison's disease, are often life threatening but fortunately rare. Unfortunately, a large number of people, especially new mothers, suffer from milder forms of fatigue caused by adrenal exhaustion. However, because their symptoms fall somewhere in the middle of the spectrum between benign mild fatigue and the life-threatening Addison's disease, medical science doesn't always focus on their needs.

? Why do new mothers experience adrenal exhaustion? In many cases, the woman comes home from the hospital to a new world of challenges, questions, and overwhelming responsibility. She feels that she must do everything herself rather than ask for help. Before long, she has used up the initial burst of energy provided by her adrenal gland. Because the responsibilities associated with parenthood don't stop when the mother is tired, her body continues to draw upon her diminishing adrenal gland output until her adrenal gland becomes exhausted.

Mild cases of adrenal exhaustion can be treated by making changes in nutrition and lifestyle, discussed below. More severe cases of this condition, referred to as Addison's Syndrome, are characterized by total exhaustion, low immunity, inability to digest food, and intolerance to noise, stress, or temperature changes, and must be immediately addressed with natural hydrocortisone therapy. Many women fall into the mild to severe category and will significantly benefit from active treatment.

What You Can Do:

* Help your partner relax. When she becomes stressed, even if it is for a good reason, her brain draws upon all that her adrenal gland has to offer. While this is helpful in the short term, it drains her body in the long term. So when she becomes agitated or wired, encourage her to breathe deeply, calm her body, and rest.

* Help your partner get more sleep. For more information about how you can help her do this, see "Sleep Deprivation & Insomnia" (page 76) and "A Parent's Guide to Adjusting to New Sleep Patterns" (page 228).

* Mild depression and anxiety often strain an adrenal gland. Help your partner lessen both. See any of the sections that address depression and anxiety in this guidebook.

* B vitamins can help a new mother manage her stress. Visit your local health food store for a vitamin B complex supplement. Encourage her to take 25 to 50 milligrams once daily with food and 100 milligrams pantothenic acid (vitamin B_5) once daily with food.

* Magnesium supplements are incredibly effective for calming anxiety and regulating the adrenal gland. Visit your local health food store for fast-absorbing magnesium, such as magnesium glycinate, magnesium gluconate, magnesium citrate, or magnesium aspartate, in capsules or sublingual (under the tongue) drops. Encourage your partner to take the dosage suggested on the bottle and slowly increase the dosage every few days. She should reduce her dosage if she feels fatigued, if her muscles feel weak, or if she experiences diarrhea. If your partner believes that she may be using too much magnesium, she can visit her physician for a blood test to evaluate the level of magnesium in her red blood cells. *If your partner has a history of kidney function problems, she should use magnesium only under the strict supervision of a physician.* Magnesium is safe for use when breastfeeding.

* Visit your local health food store for other natural remedies for stress and exhaustion, including licorice acid (ideal for exhaustion, but not agitation); Rhodiola herb; American, Russian, or Korean ginseng. These herbs help aid in both relaxation and energizing. Licorice acid should not be taken by women with high blood pressure or potassium deficiency.

* Assist your partner in gathering additional information on the subject of fatigue. One excellent source is *Tired of Being Tired: Rescue, Repair, Rejuvenate* by Nancy Deville and Jesse Lynn Hanley, M.D.

When to Get More Help:

If your partner's mild fatigue does not respond to the remedies outlined above, help her find a nutrition-oriented physician who can assist her by tailoring a program specifically for her.

If your partner appears to have a more severe form of adrenal exhaustion, help her seek a treatment program from a nutrition-oriented physician that includes natural supplements of the hormones DHEA and pregnenolone and, in extreme cases, natural hydrocortisol. The most severe form is Addison's disease. It's extremely rare, but if she shows extreme symptoms she should be referred immediately to an endocrinologist.

Depression, Memory Loss & Insomnia Due to Estrogen Deficiency

The Facts:

Immediately after delivery, a new mother's estrogen level changes from extremely high to extremely low—significantly below her pre-pregnancy level. The drop in estrogen causes some or all of the following symptoms, in mild to extreme forms:

- sleep disturbances or insomnia

- panic attacks or heart palpitations

- hot flashes or night sweats

- vaginal dryness

- memory decline or mental fogginess

- mild unhappiness or severe depression

- diminished social interest and skills

- diminished sexual desire

- diminished self-perception and care regarding appearance

- diminished desire to leave the house

These symptoms may not start right away—three weeks to six months may pass before they become noticeable.

What You Can Do:

* If you believe your partner may be estrogen deficient, bring your suspicions to her attention. Ask her if she is experiencing any of the symptoms listed above. If she says that she is, encourage her to visit her physician for a blood test that measures her estrogen level. If her estrogen level is low, the physician will probably prescribe estrogen. Even if her estrogen level

is normal or on the low end of normal, she can request estrogen in order to try to alleviate her symptoms. After all, an estrogen level that is normal for one woman may be too low for another.

* Encourage your partner to ask her physician about taking a natural form of estrogen. It is best to avoid taking synthetic estrogen. When natural estrogen is used (instead of the synthetic forms of estrogen often associated with dramatic side effects) it is usually a quick and simple process to determine whether the estrogen is helping, since she will probably feel some changes right away. On the other hand, if it turns out that the estrogen is not right for your partner, it will leave her system within a few hours. Estrogen is safe for use when breastfeeding.

! **In some women, although not many, supplementing natural estrogen may decrease the supply of breast milk.**

* Estrogen, the main "female" hormone, actually comprises *three* different types of estrogen: esteron (E1), estradiol (E2), and estriol (E3). Most physicians who prescribe estrogen recommend the use of estradiol (E2) by patch or pill. However, supplementing all three of the estrogen types found in the new mother's body—E1, E2, and E3—is optional.

* For more information on how and when to use natural estrogen, see Part Two of this guidebook, "The New Mother's Mind: Recognizing, Preventing & Treating Postpartum Depression & Mood Changes."

! **Because many doctors are not yet aware of the benefits of natural hormone supplements, most would not routinely recommend supplementing estrogen for the symptoms described above. Instead, many experienced physicians would prescribe antidepressants despite mounting evidence showing that natural forms of estrogen help to alleviate**

these symptoms. You and your partner can encourage her physician to work together with you to learn about the benefits of natural estrogen.

When to Get More Help:

If your partner's doctor refuses to consider prescribing natural estrogen, help your partner find another doctor who is more open to this type of therapy.

Anxiety & Irritability Due to Progesterone Deficiency

The Facts:

Immediately after delivery, a new mother's progesterone level drops very quickly—even more dramatically than her estrogen level does—often resulting in the following symptoms:

- ⊙ insomnia
- ⊙ agitation
- ⊙ nervousness
- ⊙ restlessness
- ⊙ panic

What You Can Do:

* If you believe your partner may be progesterone deficient, bring your suspicions to her attention. Ask her if she is experiencing any of the symptoms listed above. If she says that she is, and she believes that these symptoms are preventing her from enjoying her new motherhood, encourage her to speak to her physician about a natural progesterone prescription. Simply supplementing her diet with the progesterone she has recently lost by taking a natural form of progesterone can be incredibly effective in helping a new mother relax, remain calm, and sleep. Natural progesterone is safe for use when breastfeeding.

* For more detailed information on how to naturally supplement progesterone, see Part Two of this guidebook, "The New Mother's Mind: Recognizing, Preventing & Treating Postpartum Depression & Mood Changes."

! Because many doctors are not yet aware of the benefits of natural hormone supplements, most would not routinely recommend supplementing progesterone for the symptoms described above. Instead, many experienced physicians would prescribe antidepressants despite mounting evidence showing that natural forms of progesterone help to alleviate these symptoms. You and your partner can encourage her physician to work together to learn about the benefits of natural progesterone.

When to Get More Help:

If your partner's doctor refuses to consider prescribing natural progesterone, help your partner find another doctor who is more open to this type of therapy.

Poor Sleep Due to Melatonin Deficiency

The Facts:

Melatonin is a hormone that is essential for proper sleep. It is also an antioxidant—a substance that helps the body fight illness, like vitamin C—that has many other helpful qualities. In order to produce melatonin, the body requires darkness. Simply covering the eyes or being in a dark room is sufficient.

New mothers may become melatonin deficient if they stay up late or wake up multiple times during the night and turn on the lights. The result is that new mothers often suffer from an *inability* to fall asleep, sleep deeply, and stay asleep.

What You Can Do:

* As evening falls, keep the lights low.

* If you wake up in the middle of the night, resist the urge to turn on the light. Encourage your partner to do the same.

* Help her to attend to the baby in the middle of the night without turning on the lights—install night lights in the areas where she most often walks.

* Visit your local health food store or pharmacy for melatonin supplements in capsule or sublingual (under the tongue) drop form. Your partner can take 1 milligram one-half hour before bedtime. This dosage may be increased daily by 1 milligram but should not exceed 7 milligrams. Most people will not tolerate more than 3 milligrams. Your partner should reduce the dosage if she finds that she rises too early, experiences disturbing dreams, or wakes up feeling groggy. When purchasing your partner's melatonin, look for products that are synthetically produced rather than those extracted from animals. Melatonin supplements are safe for use when breastfeeding.

* If the new mother finds that the melatonin helps her fall asleep, but when she wakes she has trouble going back to sleep, suggest that she take half of her usual dose when she wakes during the night.

* If your partner would like to take melatonin to help her nap during the day, install blackout shades in the bedroom or purchase an inexpensive sleep mask, like those used by airplane passengers.

When to Get More Help:

If your partner continues to have trouble falling asleep despite supplementing her diet with melatonin, see "Sleep Deprivation & Insomnia" (page 76) for additional suggestions.

Hypoglycemia, or Low Blood Sugar

The Facts:

Hypoglycemia occurs when a new mother's body experiences a sharp drop in blood sugar, usually following a meal. The symptoms of hypoglycemia include:

- ⊙ agitation
- ⊙ fast heartbeat
- ⊙ faintness
- ⊙ perspiration
- ⊙ hypotension (low blood pressure)

? **Why do blood sugar levels fall? When a person consumes a meal composed mostly of carbohydrates, such as pasta, bread, rice, potato, or cereal, her body compensates by producing more insulin to process these foods and—at the end of this process—blood sugar drops.**

In new mothers, the symptoms of hypoglycemia may become more pronounced if they tend to skip meals while busy with the baby and snack on fast food and junk food that are high in carbohydrates and low on nutrition. New mothers who are particularly susceptible to hypoglycemia include vegetarians, women who gained a great deal of weight during pregnancy, and women who suffered from gestational diabetes.

? **How can you and your partner tell if she is suffering from hypoglycemia? If she feels tired, agitated, overheated, sweaty, or dizzy within two to three hours following a meal, she may be hypoglycemic.**

Hypoglycemia may be formally diagnosed by a doctor using a blood test to measure a patient's "fasting sugar and insulin levels." However, most new mothers don't have time to visit the doctor, and most doctors would simply suggest the treatments listed below. So if your partner believes that she is experiencing hypoglycemia, she may wish to try these lifestyle changes before seeing her doctor.

What You Can Do:

* Encourage your partner to evaluate her diet and eating schedule. Is she eating frequently enough throughout the day to avoid a dip in her blood sugar level? Ideally, she should eat three meals and two snacks every day—even if she believes that she doesn't have time to eat.

* What she eats is just as important as when she eats. Your partner's meals and snacks should contain very few processed carbohydrates such as bread, pasta, cereal, and starchy vegetables. The Zone and The Atkins Diet both offer low-carbohydrate eating guidelines that are appropriate for a hypoglycemic new mother. Both The Zone and The Atkins Diet are safe for breastfeeding mothers when enough protein is consumed. For more information on these diets and protein requirements, see "Ideal Postpartum Diet" (page 148).

* Visit your health food store for a supplement called alpha lipoic acid. Alpha lipoic acid is an important antioxidant that restores insulin sensitivity. Your partner may take 100 to 300 milligrams two times daily with food, and should reevaluate the condition after three months. Alpha lipoic acid is safe for use when breastfeeding.

* Also pick up a supplement called vanadium. Vanadium is a trace element that helps to restore insulin sensitivity. Your partner may take 10 to 15 milligrams three times daily on an empty stomach, and should reevaluate the condition after three months. Vanadium is safe for use when breastfeeding.

* Finally, suggest that your partner take chromium picolonate. Like vanadium, chromium picolonate is a trace element that helps to restore insulin sensitivity. Your partner may take 200 to 400 micrograms three times daily on an empty stomach, and should reevaluate the condition after three months. Chromium picolonate is safe for use when breastfeeding. Your partner may take alpha lipoic acid, vanadium, and chromium picolonate concurrently.

When to Get More Help:

If your partner's hypoglycemia symptoms do not decrease in response to the remedies listed above, encourage her to contact her physician for a blood test that measures her sugar level and insulin level after fasting.

Night Sweats

The Facts:

New mothers generally suffer from night sweats due to the drastic drop in estrogen levels immediately after delivery. Although they are most bothersome for the first few nights and tend to disappear completely within three or four weeks, night sweats can be very disruptive to a new mother's sleep and should be addressed.

! Two common methods of treating night sweats, soy estrogen treatment and black cohosh supplements, can be more problematic than helpful. Soy estrogen treatment may help alleviate your partner's hot flashes and night sweats, but, according to recent studies, it may also block the memory sites of the brain, allowing new mothers to get better sleep but at the expense of their memory! Black cohosh may provide temporary relief from night sweats, but it also prevents the body's natural estrogen from being effective and preventing a new mother from enjoying the many benefits associated with estrogen production.

What You Can Do:

* Help make your partner more comfortable by laying a soft bath towel on top of the fitted sheet on her side of the bed before she turns in for the night. The bath towel will absorb the perspiration so that she doesn't wake up in completely drenched sheets. You might also put a spare bath towel and pair of pajamas next to her bed (so she can easily change her towel and pajamas in the middle of the night) and place a hand towel and some cool water by her bedside.

When to Get More Help:

If your partner's night sweats are extreme and do not begin to subside in a few days, encourage your partner to see her physician and ask about supplementing natural estrogen. For more information, see "Depression, Memory Loss & Insomnia Due to Estrogen Deficiency" (page 99).

5 BREASTFEEDING

Beginning to Breastfeed

The Facts:

In many parts of the world, the whole issue of breastfeeding is simply considered a natural process associated with having children, unlike in the United States, where women sometimes choose not to breastfeed or have historically been instructed not to breastfeed.

Today, with the American Academy of Pediatrics's overwhelmingly enthusiastic endorsement of the health benefits associated with breastfeeding (and in response to that organization's recommendation that mothers breastfeed for at least six months to one year), more and more women are choosing to return to this method. They find it to be a simple, healthful means of feeding their baby that allows them to nurture and establish a positive bond with the child.

On the other hand, breastfeeding is not a snap. It's not easy to learn to breastfeed—teaching a baby to latch on to the breast properly and nurse efficiently can be quite difficult and frustrating, depending on the baby's temperament, appetite, and sucking technique. In addition, nursing mothers have to deal with leaking milk, engorged breasts, and sore nipples. They may also find themselves cutting activities short and sitting still for long periods throughout the day.

As her partner, anything you can do to make breastfeeding easier for her will help her feel supported and more able to enjoy breastfeeding. As a result, she will probably breastfeed the baby longer, benefiting both mother and child.

What You Can Do:

* Recognize that beginning the breastfeeding process can be frustrating. A new mother is likely to feel disappointed if she expects to be able to *instantly* feed her baby by placing his

mouth to her nipple. Unfortunately, most new mothers are not aware that breastfeeding actually involves a learning process. Disappointment and frustration over breastfeeding, combined with a drastic drop in estrogen levels after delivery, may cause your partner to become upset and feel as if she has already "failed" at motherhood. This is your moment to be understanding. Encourage her. Listen to her. Tell her that you believe in her. If she perseveres and accepts the gentle assistance of a lactation consultant, she will soon be able to provide ample nourishment to her baby.

* Once your partner gives birth, suggest that she request a professional lactation specialist employed by the hospital to watch her as she breastfeeds in order to ensure that her technique is ideal. What is an ideal technique? One that results in the baby's being fully fed each time, with little or no discomfort felt by the mother.

* Breastfeeding requires that your partner sit in one place for quite a while. Make this time more pleasant for her by stocking her favorite nursing spot with a basket or other container full of snacks, ointment, water, magazines, and a telephone.

* While your partner is breastfeeding, as was the case during her pregnancy, what she eats will affect the baby. Encourage her to eat healthy, less processed foods whenever possible—these will

be the building blocks for your baby's body and brain. Help her make healthy food choices by helping to prepare nutritious meals when processed frozen foods are the only choices at home.

* Breastfeeding mothers require a great deal of water. Encourage your partner to stay hydrated by drinking at least eight to twelve glasses of water per day.

* Be your partner's breastfeeding "point guard." Make note of her breastfeeding habits while she is out of the house. If you notice that she avoids breastfeeding while out, ask her whether there is anything you can do to make it easier for her to do so. If your partner feels shy about nursing in public situations, remind her that breastfeeding is a natural human function. Whether she chooses to nurse the baby in private or in public, assure her that her friends, her family members, and even strangers will understand. If she feels terribly uncomfortable about nursing in front of other people, offer to find her a private place to breastfeed. For example, assist her by inquiring of restaurant managers on her behalf. See "Nursing in Public" (page 135) for more information.

* If your partner feels comfortable breastfeeding in the company of friends, assist her in maintaining the level of modesty she prefers. Be mindful of whether she requires your assistance in reaching for her drink, a fallen baby blanket, etc.

* Alternatively, encourage your partner to free herself from the need to breastfeed in public by availing herself of a breast pump. Pumping her breast milk prior to leaving the house will allow her to bottle-feed your baby while in public. Offer to purchase or borrow a breast pump for her. Assist her in learning how to use the breast pump.

? How do you choose a lactation specialist? Often, a woman in your partner's family—her mother, sister, or aunt—will serve in this role. The hospital in which your partner gives birth may also offer the services of a professional lactation specialist on the day after delivery. (However, if possible, it's a good idea to take a breastfeeding class or consult a lactation specialist while your partner is still pregnant.) If you need to find a consultant after you've brought the baby home, ask friends, your pediatrician, or your partner's obstetrician for several referrals. Encourage your partner to interview these consultants over the phone prior to choosing one. She will want to choose a consultant with a breastfeeding philosophy that matches her own (e.g., breastfeeding "on demand" or in the family bed).

* If, despite your decision as a couple to breastfeed your baby, your partner decides that breastfeeding is not for her, support her and encourage her to feel confident about her choice. Respect her decision, because she probably did not make it lightly and easily. No woman should be made to feel guilty for following her instincts regarding what is right for her and her family.

When to Get More Help:

If your partner experiences problems with breastfeeding, immediately call a lactation specialist for help. Contact the hospital where your partner delivered for a referral. The lactation specialist will observe the new mother as she breastfeeds and make suggestions. Often, small changes in technique make a big difference. If done early on, such an evaluation can prevent serious discomfort and frustration on the part of your partner and your baby, and it may be the deciding factor in her struggle to continue breastfeeding.

Changes in Nipples during Pregnancy & Lactation

The Facts:

The nipple was designed for the task of breastfeeding. Nipples begin to transform in anticipation of this role during pregnancy, changing in size, firmness, toughness, and color.

The majority of these new characteristics will disappear once your partner stops breastfeeding. The size of nipples and areolae (the area around the nipple) will lessen somewhat, but the color of her nipples is likely to remain dark. Many new fathers find these changes attractive, and some find it interesting to observe their partner's body as it prepares for the important task of feeding a baby.

? Do nipples manifest these changes if your partner chooses not to breastfeed? Yes. Even if your partner never breastfeeds her nipples and areolae will still change, although their size will reduce more quickly. Her nipples will retain a darker color regardless.

What You Can Do:

Your partner may express concern about the changes in her nipples. She may have been very fond of the way her nipples looked prior to pregnancy and may now worry that their new appearance is less attractive. Reassure her that the size and shape of her nipples are likely to return to normal after pregnancy and that you find them attractive. Be patient and understanding.

When to Get More Help:

If your partner's nipples fail to become fully erect when stimulated, or if they crack or bleed, see "Inverted or Unresponsive Nipples" (page 117) or "Dry, Cracked, or Bleeding Nipples" (page 125).

Inverted or Unresponsive Nipples

The Facts:

The breast is the food delivery vehicle for your baby. As such, the nipple must be ready to deliver when the baby arrives. Inverted nipples or nipples that do not rise and harden when stimulated by touch may make breastfeeding difficult for your partner.

What You Can Do:

PRIOR TO THE ARRIVAL OF YOUR BABY:

* While it is possible to home-test for *inverted* nipples, it is better to see a lactation specialist if your partner's nipples are small and flat, rather than risk a misdiagnosis. Encourage your partner to see her physician and a lactation specialist for "treatment" before the baby arrives.

* You or your partner can test her nipples to see if they are *unresponsive* by stimulating them. Responsive nipples will harden and rise above the surface of the breast when stimulated. A lactation specialist can help to sensitize unresponsive nipples before the baby arrives.

* A suckling baby can be very hard on nipples that were previously only caressed. Help your partner's nipples prepare for the work ahead of them by encouraging her to wear a T-shirt without a bra a few hours each day. The constant friction will toughen the skin on the nipples.

* If your partner has unresponsive nipples, suggest that she sensitize them by taking a *warm* (not hot) wet hand towel and lightly brush the nipples for a minute every few days. Don't overdo it.

? Does breast size affect the ability to breastfeed? No. The size of the breast generally has no correlation to milk production. In fact, women with AA-cup breasts can feed a baby with the same success as a woman with DD-cup breasts!

FOLLOWING THE ARRIVAL OF YOUR BABY:

* If you and your partner did not prepare her unresponsive or inverted nipples prior to the arrival of your baby, make a point of addressing this issue as soon as possible. The longer you wait, the more difficult breastfeeding will become and the more complications and discomfort your partner may experience. Once your baby is born, see a lactation specialist for a more individual approach to treating your partner's inverted or unresponsive nipples.

When to Get More Help:

If your partner's nipples are inverted or unresponsive and the remedies listed above do not help, seek the help of a lactation specialist. Ideally, you will consult a lactation specialist several months prior to the arrival of your baby.

Painful Breast Swelling, or Engorgement

The Facts:

It is common for breasts to become engorged and painful after delivery.

What is breast engorgement? A breast becomes engorged when it has accumulated too much breast milk due to delayed or insufficient breastfeeding. The breast feels hard and is painful. When the breast is engorged for some period of time and the milk is not drained from the breast, either by breastfeeding or pumping, the milk ducts can become plugged, which can lead to a breast infection.

New mothers may experience breast engorgement when they are beginning to breastfeed. Mothers may also experience engorged breasts when they attempt to stop breastfeeding or if they breastfeed only intermittently.

? Did you know that breast tissue extends to the underarms? Most men and women don't. For this reason, it is common for women whose breasts swell in pregnancy and especially after delivery to call their obstetricians with fears that they have developed a cancerous lump under their arm. If your partner fits this description, don't worry! Encourage her to call her doctor to confirm that breast milk is the only substance growing in her underarms.

What You Can Do:

* If your partner believes that she has plugged breast ducts, see "Plugged Breast Ducts" (page 129).

* If your partner believes that she has a breast infection, see "Breast Infection, or Mastitis" (page 131).

- To help your partner avoid breast pain due to delayed breast-feeding, make it easier for her to breastfeed at her regular feeding times. This may require you to assist her in excusing herself from social obligations, finding a quiet place to breast-feed, or waking up the baby if he or she is sleeping through a feeding.

- To help your partner avoid breast pain due to engorgement when she (or the baby) reduces the amount she breastfeeds or when the baby skips a feeding, suggest that she use her breast pump to express her milk, thereby relieving her discomfort.

- You may also help her by giving her a cold compress or ice pack, which she can apply to her breasts to relieve pain and swelling related to engorgement. Alternatively, if her breasts are so engorged that the baby has trouble latching on, give her a warm compress or hot water bottle to apply to her breasts just before nursing.

When to Get More Help:

If mild breast pain or breast engorgement causes breasts to become red, very painful, or tender, or if she develops a fever, call her physician. Your partner may have developed an infection in one or both of her breasts (although it is uncommon for infection to occur in both breasts at once).

Breast Milk Production

The Facts:

Many new mothers express concern that the amount of breast milk they produce may not be enough to feed their baby. How can a new mother or father determine if the baby is getting enough milk?

Simply listen to your baby. If your baby is gaining weight according to your pediatrician's expectations, if he becomes calm and doesn't cry immediately after feedings, and if he has six to eight wet diapers per day, then your baby is likely getting enough milk.

What You Can Do:

* With your partner's permission, invite a lactation specialist to watch her breastfeed in the hospital or at home during the first few days. The lactation specialist will help your partner correct small technique problems early on, thereby helping her to increase her milk supply, or will confirm that her milk supply is sufficient to feed the baby.

* If the baby is not getting enough milk, it may be because your partner is not nursing long enough or often enough. One of the surest ways to increase milk supply is to simply nurse more frequently or longer. Breastfeeding works on a supply-and-demand basis—the more the breasts are called upon to produce milk, the more milk they will produce. Simply adding a few minutes to each feeding or shortening the time between feedings by fifteen or thirty minutes during the day can increase a mother's milk supply.

* Help your partner get enough sleep at night and downtime during the day. Exhaustion can reduce a new mother's milk supply.

* Encourage your partner to increase the amount of water she drinks. A breastfeeding mother should drink at least eight to twelve glasses of water daily.

* Help your partner get enough protein and essential fats in her diet—see the minimum protein and fat requirements outlined in "Ideal Postpartum Diet" (page 148).

* Several months into breastfeeding, the growth of your baby and his demand for milk may exceed a new mother's production ability. Encourage your partner to discuss this with her physician and a lactation specialist to ensure that her breastfeeding technique continues to be effective. Additionally, pay a visit to your baby's pediatrician. If he or she is satisfied with your baby's weight, then your partner's milk production is sufficient.

* Remind your partner that—while it does require some instruction (from a mother, a sister, or a lactation specialist)—breastfeeding is an essential part of our evolution as a species. Nature does not intend for the process of breastfeeding to be impossible to achieve—if so, we would have already died off! Encourage your partner to relax and consult with a woman who has gone through this process before. Feelings of frustration are normal and should be listened to with compassion. Remind her that her body already knows what to do and has been waiting to play out this biological role since she was fed as a baby.

When to Get More Help:

If your partner believes that she has a mechanical problem with breastfeeding, contact the lactation specialist who helped your partner in the hospital or call your partner's physician for a referral.

If you and your partner believe that your baby is not receiving enough milk, consult your baby's pediatrician, who will confirm whether your baby is growing at the expected rate.

Maintaining Hydration

The Facts:

Maintaining proper hydration is the key to promoting fast healing and bountiful milk production after delivery. Sufficient water *and* minerals are essential for optimal body function in general, and a fully hydrated woman has more energy, better concentration, and a faster recovery from childbirth. Her body more quickly rids itself of the medications it was subjected to during labor and delivery. And, because she feels better, she can make better food choices, which will help her return to her pre-pregnancy weight.

? Why are mineral levels as important as water levels? They are important for the same reason athletes drink sports beverages and doctors recommend electrolyte-rich fluids to ailing patients. Minerals such as sodium, magnesium, iron, potassium, and copper are essential to maintaining proper body functions. Although spring and artesian waters can supply our bodies with many of these minerals, filtered water may have had these elements removed. The next time you purchase bottled water, inspect the nutritional information chart on the label—do you see a column of zeros? If so, the water you've purchased does not contain the minerals your body requires. To ensure that you, your partner, and your baby ingest these beneficial elements, create a natural electrolyte-rich sports drink by adding sea salt and honey to your water. Start by adding small amounts of sea salt and honey and increase both to suit your partner's taste.

New mothers, especially those who are breastfeeding, can easily become dehydrated. Symptoms of dehydration include:

- ⊙ elevated body temperature

- ⊙ dry skin, especially facial skin that appears wrinkled

- ⊙ fatigue

- headache

- forgetfulness

- dizziness

- dark urine and less frequent urination

- irritability

What You Can Do:

* Encourage your partner to drink at least eight to twelve glasses of water per day. She should drink more during warm weather, on days when the baby nurses more frequently, and when she exercises. Place a pitcher of water at your partner's bedside and keep it filled with fresh water while she is recovering from childbirth and breastfeeding.

* Visit your local pharmacy for a mineral-rich solution that will help a mineral-deficient new mother feel better.

* If your partner indicates that she would like to better control her food choices, encourage her to drink two glasses of mineral-rich water prior to eating and then another two just after eating.

* If she would like to become more active, encourage her to drink more water. A properly hydrated new mother is less likely to be tired and more likely to have enough energy for exercise.

When to Get More Help:

If your partner has been vomiting or has had diarrhea for more than eight hours and is unable to keep any liquids in her system, or if she feels faint, call her physician. He or she may need to administer aggressive medical intervention.

Dry, Cracked, or Bleeding Nipples

The Facts:

Especially during the first few weeks, breastfeeding can be hard on nipples that previously were handled only lightly. New nursing mothers can expect to experience some tenderness for the first few days. This will recede as the nipple skin becomes tougher. However, nipples may become dry or cracked if the mother's breastfeeding technique requires adjustment.

Sore, dry, cracked nipples are likely to result if the baby is positioned improperly, is sucking only on the protruding part of the nipple and not taking the whole areola in his mouth, or is not releasing the nipple properly. Women with flat or inverted nipples may have trouble teaching their baby to latch on correctly. Positioning the baby correctly and practicing proper nursing techniques can prevent or minimize soreness, no matter what kind of nipples your partner has.

If your partner has flat or inverted nipples or consistently has trouble getting the baby to latch on correctly, she will probably need the guidance of a professional lactation specialist or mother, sister, or close friend with breastfeeding experience. See "Inverted or Unresponsive Nipples" (page 117) for more information.

And even if your partner is doing everything right, sensitive skin and nipples and an over-enthusiastic baby may result in sore nipples for new and repeat mothers in the first few weeks of breastfeeding.

? Is it necessary for your partner to stop breastfeeding if her nipples are dry, cracked, or bleeding? No, as long as the pain of breastfeeding with nipples in this condition does not prevent her from doing so. In fact, stopping nursing because of nipple pain will likely lead to more breast pain, from engorgement.

What You Can Do:

* Attend a breastfeeding class with your partner or consult a lactation specialist during pregnancy in order to ensure that her nipples do not require any additional attention prior to beginning breastfeeding. After all, every woman is built differently, and some women's nipples require some preparation in order to make breastfeeding easier once your baby arrives. Most of these preparations can be done very easily. A breastfeeding consultation will also provide you both with a quick primer on how breastfeeding works.

* Help your partner "toughen" her nipples throughout her pregnancy to prepare them for breastfeeding. Encourage her to wear a T-shirt without a bra for a few hours a day or use a wet towel to lightly rub her nipples for a few minutes every day.

* Once your partner gives birth, suggest that she request a professional lactation specialist employed by the hospital to watch her as she breastfeeds in order to ensure that her technique is ideal. What is an ideal technique? One that results in the baby's being fully fed each time, with little or no discomfort felt by the mother.

* If the nipples begin to get sore, suggest that she limit your baby's breastfeeding sessions to five minutes per side during the first few days, in order to allow her nipples to gradually adjust to their new role. She should begin with the breast that was not suckled last.

* Breast milk, *particularly* colostrum, the substance secreted from the nipple for the first three to five days after the baby is born, has antiseptic and healing properties. Prior to feeding, suggest that she gently squeeze her breast and rub the colostrum or breast milk around the nipple. Repeat after breastfeeding.

* Small bumps on the areola (the area around the nipple) secrete a mild, natural antiseptic substance that keeps the nipple clean. Soap removes this antiseptic substance, so you may want to suggest that your partner avoid using soap on her nipples.

TREATMENT:

* At the first sign of dry, cracking, or bleeding nipples, contact a lactation specialist.

* To treat the dry and cracked area, visit your pharmacy or health food store for one of the following products:

   ○ **Colostrum cream:** This cream is produced from cows' colostrum and is similar to the colostrum produced by your partner's breasts in the first few days after delivery. Look for colostrum cream derived from organically raised cows. Encourage your partner to apply enough cream to cover the whole nipple two to six times daily, rubbing until fully absorbed. Colostrum cream is safe for the baby and does not need to be wiped off before nursing.

   ○ **Evening primrose oil:** A capsule may be opened and spread on the nipple two to six times daily. Evening primrose oil is safe for the baby and does not need to be wiped off before nursing.

   ○ **Vitamin E oil:** A capsule may be opened and spread on the nipple two to six times daily. Your partner should gently rub until the oil is fully absorbed. Vitamin E oil is safe for the baby and does not need to be wiped off before nursing.

- **Ointments with olive oil, bee extract, and royal jelly:**
  These ointments may be applied to the nipple two to six
  times daily. Your partner should gently rub until the ointment is fully absorbed. These types of ointments are safe
  for the baby and do not need to be wiped off before
  nursing.

When to Get More Help:

If your partner's nipple pain is so severe that it prevents her from
breastfeeding, suggest that she contact her obstetrician or a lactation specialist to find out about tools that can be used to protect the nipple while it heals.

Plugged Breast Ducts

The Facts:

Milk ducts commonly become plugged up or blocked. When this occurs, new mothers experience the following symptoms:

- ⊙ pain in the area of the blocked milk duct

- ⊙ temporary fever

- ⊙ redness on the skin of the breast (in some cases)

Although a plugged breast duct is painful, it is less problematic than breast infection—a possible result of a plugged duct. The treatments outlined below are aimed at preventing a plugged duct from developing into a breast infection and may help treat breast infection in its early stages.

? Should your partner stop breastfeeding if a breast duct becomes plugged? Not at all. A new mother *should* continue to breastfeed despite this condition, *especially from the plugged side.*

What You Can Do:

* Encourage your partner to frequently breastfeed, pump, or do both from the painful breast.

* Next to breastfeeding, breast massage is the most effective means of unplugging breast ducts. If your partner so desires, you can assist her in massaging the painful breast. Firmly stroke the area of the duct from the outside of breast toward the nipple in the immediate area of the plugged duct.

* Give your partner a warm compress to apply to the affected breast just before breastfeeding and massaging it. This is an effective means of unclogging plugged ducts, especially when done in conjunction with massage.

* Encourage your partner to get extra rest and take in extra fluids. A breastfeeding mother should consume a minimum of eight to twelve glasses of water per day.

* Also recommend that she vary her nursing positions. When held in some nursing positions, many babies do not drain every milk duct completely, leaving particular areas of the breast still full at the end of the feeding. If the mother varies the way she holds the baby while nursing (e.g., alternating between the football hold and the cradle hold), all of her ducts will be emptied more often, making plugged ducts less severe or less likely.

* Plugged ducts sometimes develop as a result of a slightly ineffective nursing technique. You and your partner might consult a lactation specialist to make sure your baby is positioned and latching on correctly.

* Additionally, natural anti-inflammatory medications may also help manage the breast pain associated with plugged ducts. Visit your local health food store for echinacea, goldenseal, vitamin C, and beta 1-3, 1-6 glucan, all of which can be taken at once. Your partner should use these as directed. While some of these natural supplements are not appropriate for pregnant women, they are all safe for use when breastfeeding.

* Other natural remedies that may help manage plugged ducts include homeopathic antibacterial medications, sold in sublingual (under the tongue) drop form at health food stores. Encourage your partner to use as directed, four to six times daily.

When to Get More Help:

If your partner's plugged ducts do not respond to the remedies described above, contact her physician. Alternatively, if she develops a fever over 101°F or if the painful area of her breast becomes red and swollen, contact her physician.

Breast Infection, or Mastitis

The Facts:

Breast infection, or mastitis, may occur as a result of several factors, including plugged milk ducts, restrictive bras (or bras with underwire), or a skin infection of cracked or bleeding nipples. The symptoms of an infected or inflamed breast include:

- pain

- redness

- swelling

- fever that exceeds 101°F

The pain, redness, and swelling usually appear on only part of the breast, radiating from the nipple out in a triangular pattern. These symptoms may be difficult to distinguish from the symptoms of plugged milk ducts. How do you differentiate the two? A plugged breast duct responds immediately to the treatments outlined in the "Plugged Breast Ducts" section of this guidebook (page 129); breast infection does not.

Breast infection should be treated early and aggressively in order to prevent the condition from progressing to breast abscess.

? Should your partner stop breastfeeding if her breast becomes infected? Not at all. A new mother *should* continue to breastfeed despite her infection, *especially from the infected side.*

What You Can Do:

PREVENTION:

* Encourage your partner to wash her hands prior to handling her nipple and keep the area around her nipple as clean and dry as possible.

* Breast milk, *particularly* colostrum, the substance secreted from the nipple for the first three to five days after the baby is born, has antiseptic and healing properties. Suggest that, prior to feeding, she gently squeeze her breast and rub the colostrum or breast milk around the nipple. Repeat after breastfeeding.

* See "Plugged Breast Ducts" (page 129) for additional preventive measures.

TREATMENT:

* Once infection is identified, the condition is treated with antibiotic medication. In order to prevent the development of a yeast infection incident to the use of antibiotics, visit your local health food store for *Lactobacillus acidophilus* and *Bacillus bifidus*. Encourage your partner to take these supplements as directed on the days she takes antibiotics. *Lactobacillus acidophilus* and *Bacillus bifidus* are safe for use when breastfeeding.

When to Get More Help:

If your partner believes that her breast has become infected, contact her physician immediately in order to prevent the condition from progressing to breast abscess.

If, despite antibiotic treatment, her fever, pain, or swelling persists or the redness spreads, contact her physician again.

Nipple Thrush, or Yeast Infection in the Nipple

The Facts:

For a variety of reasons, some babies are prone to developing a yeast infection, or "thrush," in the mouth and diaper area. When a newborn breastfeeds, it is common for this yeast infection to spread to the mother's nipple, causing the nipple to become

- cracked or flaky

- itchy

- irritated

- swollen or puffy

Nursing causes the infection to transfer back and forth between the nipple and the baby's mouth. The discomfort associated with nipple thrush can affect your partner's ability to breastfeed.

What You Can Do:

* If your partner is experiencing the symptoms of nipple thrush, she will need to be treated with antifungal medication. Simultaneously, your baby's mouth and diaper area must also be treated for thrush in order to avoid reinfection. Encourage your partner to call her physician and the baby's pediatrician so that medical treatment can begin immediately.

* Visit your local pharmacy for a variety of over-the-counter anti-yeast creams, to be used according to her physician's recommendations.

* Alternatively, visit your local health food store for ointments with an oregano-oil or grape-seed-extract base. Both of these substances have very strong anti-yeast properties. A small amount of ointment should be rubbed onto the affected nipple

after every breastfeeding session. Because both of these oint-ments have extremely strong scents and tastes, your partner must wash them off her nipples prior to breastfeeding. These ointments may be used together.

* Alternatively, visit your local health food store for colostrum cream, an effective antiseptic that will help your partner's nip-ple heal. Apply liberally onto the nipple every few hours.

* You can also pick up zinc oxide cream, a product that helps to promote nipple healing. It is not necessary to wash zinc cream off prior to breastfeeding.

* Some folk remedies involve applying yogurt to the nipples in order to fight the infection with healthy bacteria known as *Lactobacillus acidophilus*. Unfortunately, the majority of yogurts in supermarkets have a very low level of these friendly bacteria. Check the yogurt labels, and choose an unsweetened, unflavored type that has a high level of healthy bacteria.

* Encourage your partner to avoid using soap on her nipples— especially antibacterial soaps, which can be harsh and are likely to irritate her skin.

* If possible, encourage your partner to "air out" her nipples. Exposure to air and sun assists in the healing of this condition.

* Remind your partner that consuming yeast, sugar, and starch promotes the development of yeast that causes nipple thrush. She may want to limit her and the baby's consumption of foods containing these elements.

When to Get More Help:

If your partner's condition does not respond to the remedies out-lined above, encourage her to contact her physician or the baby's pediatrician for further treatment.

Nursing in Public

The Facts:

Some new mothers feel uncomfortable about the prospect of breastfeeding away from home and in public. Sometimes she may feel shy about the possibility of exposing her breasts to friends and strangers, and other times she may worry that she may be making *others* uncomfortable. Both of these concerns should be respected.

Generally, as the new mother and baby become more skilled at nursing, they spend less time trying to latch on and more time peacefully feeding. The mother becomes more comfortable with this bodily function and, as a result, she gradually finds it easier and less stressful to breastfeed in public.

A problem arises when a new mother avoids leaving the house with her baby so that she doesn't have to confront the issue of public breastfeeding or to avoid breastfeeding while they are out. Women who avoid leaving home are less likely to resume their regular activities and exercise and may begin to feel isolated from the outside world. Those who avoid breastfeeding while they are away from home experience discomfort from swollen or engorged breasts and stress from dealing with a hungry, unhappy baby.

What You Can Do:

* Remind your partner that breastfeeding is a natural human function and that, no matter where she chooses to breastfeed, friends, family members, and even strangers will understand.

* Make note of your partner's breastfeeding habits while she is out of the house. If you notice that she avoids breastfeeding while out, ask her whether there is anything you can do to make it easier for her to do so. Perhaps she has met with

disapproval from strangers—or even from family members—and requires you to "go to bat" for her with others occasionally.

* Many books on breastfeeding offer tricks and solutions for nursing discreetly in public. Consider visiting your favorite bookseller for a few of these titles.

* In order to make public breastfeeding easier for her, offer to find her a private place to breastfeed. For example, assist her by inquiring of restaurant managers on her behalf, or help your partner to excuse herself from the company of friends by asking your host or hostess about a private room where she can nurse the baby.

* If your partner feels comfortable breastfeeding in the company of friends, assist her in maintaining the level of modesty she prefers. Some women prefer to cover the baby's suckling with a baby blanket or shawl. Be mindful of whether she requires your assistance if this blanket or any other needed item falls beyond her reach.

* Maternity stores carry many types of shirts, dresses, and bras designed specifically to help nursing mothers feed their babies discreetly. Invite your partner to go shopping with you and help her find nursing clothes and bras that she finds attractive, comfortable, and easy to operate.

* If, after a month or two (when mother and baby have established a good nursing relationship), your partner has not begun to get over her discomfort with nursing in public, she may choose to pump her breast milk prior to leaving the house so that she can bottle-feed your baby while in public. Offer to purchase, rent, or borrow a breast pump for her. Pumps can often be rented at hospital lactation centers or maternity stores. Assist her in learning how to use the breast pump. See "Breastfeeding & Pumping When She Returns to Work" (page 141) for more information about breast pumps.

When to Get More Help:

If you find that your partner's discomfort with breastfeeding in public prevents her from leaving the house, or if it causes her to avoid feeding her hungry baby and then experience breast pain from engorgement, encourage her to contact a lactation specialist for assistance in learning how to nurse discreetly.

Concerns about Being Replaced by Your Baby

The Facts:

Breastfeeding is a natural and essential part of bringing children into the world. Despite this, new fathers may feel a bit jealous of this new little person who is suddenly monopolizing your partner's breasts, which had previously been reserved for you. These feelings are common. However, it is a good idea to examine and discuss with your partner both your concerns about breastfeeding and her attitude about breastfeeding. If you don't know where to begin your discussion, look over the questions below. Your responses should give you plenty to go on.

- ⊙ Will breastfeeding always take priority above all else? Specifically, will breastfeeding take priority over our intimacy?

- ⊙ How do I feel about breastfeeding in general?

- ⊙ Do I envy the fact that another person has access to my partner's breasts?

- ⊙ How does intimate contact with lactating breasts make me feel?

- ⊙ How do I feel about my partner breastfeeding in public?

- ⊙ How do I feel about my partner breastfeeding in front of my friends?

What You Can Do:

FOR THE NEW FATHER:

* Many men feel uncomfortable sharing "unfatherly" feelings about breastfeeding. Unfortunately, failing to share these

concerns may inadvertently create miscommunication—and ultimately a rift between you and your partner. Don't allow your relationship to suffer in this way. Although you may feel awkward, force yourself to address these concerns with your partner.

* By the same token, be understanding about your partner's feelings about breastfeeding. Particularly in the beginning, your partner may feel uncertain about her new role and may feel compelled to breastfeed whenever your baby cries—even if it requires her to curtail your intimate time together. Give her room to experiment with various breastfeeding routines and try to set aside your frustrations about this new challenge in your relationship.

FOR THE NEW MOTHER:

* Don't assume that your partner's feelings about breastfeeding are all positive. Generally, new fathers are instinctively supportive, but many still need to share their feelings about this change in your relationship. Encourage your partner to express his "inappropriate" feelings. If possible or reasonable, adjust your behavior or routines to take these feelings into account. By opening the subject of breastfeeding, you strengthen your relationship and partnership as parents.

* In some cases, new mothers feel as if they are merely "baby-feeding machines" to their partners. They may feel alienated because they see that much of the affection they once enjoyed is now being showered upon the little one; they feel replaced. Generally, new fathers do not realize how their partners feel or that they have favored their child over their partner. Consider broaching this subject in a calm, loving manner. Explain to your partner that the very best parenting begins with parents who share an affectionate relationship.

When to Get More Help:

FOR THE NEW FATHER:

If you believe that your partner is being insensitive to or unreasonable about your feelings regarding breastfeeding, or if you believe that your partner's breastfeeding goals are disrupting your ability to resume your life together as lovers, make an effort to address these concerns with her as early as possible. Don't assume that your concerns will pass on their own. If you find that you are uncomfortable speaking with your partner about this subject, or if you find that she does not respond to your attempts to discuss this subject, consider seeking the assistance of a family therapist or clergyperson.

FOR THE NEW MOTHER:

If you believe that the way your partner expresses his feelings about your breastfeeding is unreasonable, make every effort to address his reactions. For example, you may feel that your partner is being unreasonable if he does any of the following:

- becomes upset when you get up to breastfeed in the midst of intimacy and refuses to resume intimacy when you return

- refuses to converse with you after you get up to attend to the baby

- demands that you end a breastfeeding session to attend to a task that does not require immediate attention

- insists that you stop breastfeeding altogether before you are ready

If your attempts to discuss his feelings are unsuccessful, consider seeking the assistance of a family therapist or clergyperson.

Breastfeeding & Pumping When She Returns to Work

The Facts:

The American Academy of Pediatrics has stated that breast milk is the "optimal form of nutrition for infants" and recommends that new mothers breastfeed for the first six months to one year of their baby's life. However, many new mothers are required to return to work far sooner than six months, making it impossible to continue to breastfeed their baby every two to four hours, and effectively ending breastfeeding. But this needn't be the case.

Fortunately, developments in breast pump technology have made it possible for working mothers to continue to provide breast milk for their babies during working hours.

> ! Your partner does not need to wait until she returns to work to use her breast pump. Consider encouraging her to begin pumping occasionally once the baby is settled in a comfortable, effective nursing routine (usually after three to four weeks). As a result, you, other family members, and babysitters will be able to feed the baby with a bottle, thereby giving the new mother some freedom.

What You Can Do:[1]

* Help your partner obtain a good breast pump. A good breast pump can make the difference in allowing a woman to continue breastfeeding. Many women have given up breastfeeding in frustration over an inefficient or painful breast pump. Ask your friends and read consumer reports regarding the best breast pumps; the most expensive breast pump is not always the one you want. You may buy or borrow a breast pump or

---

1 Source: Barbara Philipp, "Encouraging Patients to Use a Breast Pump," *Contemporary OB/GYN* 88–100. January 2003, Volume 48, Issue 1.

rent one on a monthly basis. Contact the lactation center at the hospital where your partner gave birth for more information; you may be able to buy or rent one there.

* Prior to her return to work, encourage her to build up a supply of breast milk. She should freeze milk in 2- to 4-ounce plastic bags specifically made to hold breast milk. Small amounts are easier to thaw than large amounts, and less is wasted if your baby does not finish the milk in the package.

? How long does breast milk last? Refrigerated breast milk lasts for only about eight days; breast milk that is frozen in a conventional freezer with a door that is separate from that of the refrigerator can remain frozen for three to six months. Breast milk stored in a horizontal deep freezer can last six to twelve months.

? How do you defrost frozen breast milk? Simply move the breast milk packet from the freezer to the refrigerator to defrost the milk over a twelve-hour period. For a faster thaw, place the packet in a cup or bowl on the kitchen counter or run tepid water over the packet. *Do not microwave breast milk.* Defrosted breast milk may separate or acquire a slightly yellow color. Neither of these characteristics affects the nutritive value of the breast milk. Milk that has separated should be swirled before feeding.

* In the weeks prior to her return to work, encourage her to start introducing a bottle of breast milk once a day. If your baby refuses to take the bottle from her mother, you can give it a try—just make sure the mother is out of the baby's sight. Often, receiving the bottle from someone other than the mother does the trick. Alternatively, start off by offering your baby expressed breast milk in an infant medicine spoon or, if your child is older, in a "sippy" cup with a lid.

* Encourage your partner to plan for a smooth back-to-work transition. Suggest that she ease into her reduced breast-

feeding schedule by working only two days during her first week back.

* Support her as she makes this big transition back to work, which is a challenge in itself. Adding a new component, pumping—not to mention her anxiety and sadness at being away from the baby—is likely to make this transition more difficult. Help her anticipate and prepare for the challenges of those first few weeks back at work. Reassure her that she is doing a great job, and that this new balancing act is likely to get easier.

* Once back at work, your partner will have to take periodic pumping breaks every four to six hours in order to avoid experiencing the discomfort and leakage associated with breast engorgement. Many states now require that employers provide working mothers with time during the day to pump. Suggest that she speak to her supervisor in advance regarding her plans so that she can create a pumping schedule that works for everyone involved.

* Operating a breast pump requires privacy and a comfortable place to sit. It may also require an electrical outlet. Many companies provide a lactation room for this purpose. Alternatively, a woman who has a private office might ask for a lock to be installed or arrange for a "Do Not Disturb Mother at Work" sign that she can hang on her door during pumping breaks. Suggest that your partner talk with her supervisor about such arrangements.

* Your partner will need a place to refrigerate her pumped milk at work and a means of transporting it. She'll want to store it, clearly marked, in the refrigerator at work. For her trips home, present her with a small, lightweight, collapsible cooler and a couple of blue ice packs to keep breast milk cool.

* A new mother's milk-ejection reflex can be triggered by hearing her baby cry, smelling her baby's clothing, glancing at her baby's picture, or simply thinking about her baby. Help her

collect items that will trigger this reflex and encourage her to keep these items in her breast pump bag. Alternatively, make an audio recording of your baby crying. Then, when she starts pumping, your partner will have items on hand that can help her focus on a mental image of the baby. As a result she will be able to express milk faster, allowing her to return to work more quickly and making it more likely that she will continue to express milk.

* To help her minimize pumping breaks, suggest that your partner breastfeed just before she leaves for work (or drops the baby off at day care) and as soon as she returns home.

* If, despite your planning as a team, your partner chooses to stop breastfeeding, support her and encourage her to feel confident about her choice. Respect her decision, because she probably did not make it lightly and easily. No woman should feel guilty when making such a personal choice.

When to Get More Help:

If your partner is having trouble pumping, suggest that she contact a lactation specialist for a brief tutorial. The specialist will observe your partner's use of the breast pump and help correct common mistakes in technique. Often, receiving small pointers makes all the difference.

She's Ready to Stop Breastfeeding

The Facts:

The American Academy of Pediatrics recommends that new mothers breastfeed for the first six months to one year of your baby's life. The length of time your partner continues breastfeeding depends on your baby's consumption, your partner's milk supply, her schedule, and her feelings regarding breastfeeding. Whether she chooses to stop at one month or one year, your support of this decision and assistance in the process will be greatly appreciated by your partner.

? Did you know that it is often physically painful for new mothers to stop breastfeeding abruptly? Nature devised an effective system to remind mothers to breastfeed frequently—every few hours, depending on how often the baby usually nurses, the mother's breasts fill with milk. If she does not nurse the baby, thereby releasing the milk, her breasts will become engorged and painful. When a new mother decides to stop breastfeeding, this "alarm clock" can cause significant pain and discomfort for several days.

What You Can Do:

* Support your partner and encourage her to feel confident about her choice to stop breastfeeding. Respect her decision, because she probably did not make it lightly and easily. No woman should feel guilty when making such a personal choice.

* If your partner gradually increases the length of time between breastfeeding sessions, she will painlessly and naturally stop the breastfeeding process. Between nursing sessions, formula or solid food (for older babies) can be given. The majority of women stop breastfeeding in this gradual fashion.

* To help your partner avoid breast pain due to engorgement if she stops breastfeeding abruptly, help her *tightly* wrap an Ace bandage around her breasts. The bandage should be left in place for forty-eight hours. Her breasts will likely not become engorged once the bandage is removed. During this time, suggest that she decrease the amount of water she drinks by 50 percent and increase her consumption of diuretic foods. See "Water Retention: Swollen Feet, Ankles & Hands" (page 34) for supplement suggestions.

When to Get More Help:

If your partner attempts to stop breastfeeding abruptly and experiences severe pain and fever despite implementing the recommendations described above, see "Painful Breast Swelling, or Engorgement" (page 119) and contact her physician.

If your partner is experiencing feelings of guilt regarding her decision to stop breastfeeding despite your support and reassurance, encourage her to talk about her feelings with another mother who has recently stopped breastfeeding.

6 LONG-TERM RECOVERY

Ideal Postpartum Diet

The Facts:

The ideal postpartum diet is similar to the healthy, varied diet your partner probably followed during pregnancy, with a few modifications. Eating a variety of fresh fruits and vegetables, whole-grain breads and cereals, and sources of protein is essential for a new mother's healing, energy, and milk supply. Following nutritional guidelines during and after pregnancy will help the new mother lose weight safely, avoid problems in subsequent pregnancies, and prevent the eventual onset of conditions such as adult diabetes.

Her postpartum diet may differ from her pregnancy diet in a few ways:

- She may now consume large, deep-sea fish such as tuna, halibut, and swordfish.

- She may now consume deli meats and unpasteurized cheeses such as blue cheese.

- She may reduce her overall food consumption gradually, keeping in mind calorie requirements if she is breast-feeding.

New mothers commonly ask, "How quickly will I get back to my 'normal' size?" The answer depends on the woman's diet and exercise level. Few women automatically shrink back to their pre-pregnancy size without paying some attention to what, how much, and how often they eat.

! While new fathers should certainly participate in creating a healthy diet for the whole family, they should let their partners take charge of their own weight loss. New fathers should not nag their partners to lose weight—it's probably best, in fact, to just avoid the subject altogether. A new mother is likely to feel sensitive about her appearance already and will be more likely to begin feeling better about herself if she feels completely accepted by her partner.

What You Can Do:

Following the diet guidelines below will speed up post-pregnancy weight loss while providing ample nutrition for your partner and for your baby, if she breastfeeds.

* The best thing a new mother can do in order to get back to her pre-pregnancy weight is to breastfeed. Discuss this with your partner to determine whether breastfeeding is right for your family.

* New mothers should avoid food and drinks (including sodas) with "empty" calories and artificial colors and preservatives. Why? By avoiding foods that contain chemicals for the liver to process, a new mother will allow her liver to focus on the immediate task at hand—flushing out the excess chemicals associated with the pregnancy and birth.

* In the first six weeks, *and at all times while breastfeeding,* new mothers should refrain from using any diet aids to assist them in losing weight, including those that claim to inhibit the absorption of food. Many diet aids contain stimulants that can have an unfavorable effect on the recovering mother and new baby.

GUIDELINES FOR NEW MOTHERS WHO BREASTFEED:

* Women who are breastfeeding should modify the suggestions given below to include *no less* than 1,200 to 1,600 calories per day, including 60 to 70 grams of protein.

* If your partner notices a correlation between a decrease in milk production and a decrease in calorie intake (evident when she pumps less milk than usual or the baby still seems hungry after nursing), suggest that she increase her intake of fats and

proteins. If increasing protein and fat consumption doesn't boost her milk supply, help her arrange to consult with a lactation specialist.

IF YOUR PARTNER BELIEVES HER WEIGHT WAS IDEAL PRIOR TO HER PREGNANCY:

* Encourage your partner to ask herself to evaluate her weight and physical shape prior to her pregnancy. If she believes that she was at her ideal weight, then she should return to the diet and activity level she maintained prior to her pregnancy. However, caution her to recognize that during her first days back she will not be able to return to the peak level of exercise she enjoyed. After all, as a new mother she is likely to be sleep deprived—a fact that in itself would prevent her from resuming her previous level of exercise! Encourage her to work up to her pre-pregnancy level and be realistic along the way in order to avoid injury.

* If your partner would like to speed weight loss but does not have many calories to cut from her diet (because she doesn't eat much to begin with), suggest that she forget about counting calories and focus on making better food choices, cutting down on starchy vegetables (see below) and processed carbohydrates (see below) and substituting sources of protein and healthy fats.

IF YOUR PARTNER BELIEVES SHE WAS OVER HER IDEAL WEIGHT PRIOR TO HER PREGNANCY:

* Encourage her to eat less of the following foods and drinks:

  ⊙ processed carbohydrates, such as breads, pastas, and cereals

  ⊙ grains, such as rice, wheat, oats, and barley

  ⊙ starchy fruits and vegetables, such as potatoes, sweet potatoes, corn, beets, carrots, and bananas

- ⊙ large beans, such as fava beans and kidney beans, *excluding* lentils and soy beans

- ⊙ juices and dried fruits

- ⊙ alcohol, including beer and wine

✳ Encourage her to limit her consumption of fresh fruit to those fruits with a low glycemic index, such as berries, cherries, apples, oranges, and grapefruits.

✳ Encourage her to consume 50 to 70 grams of protein per day. (Dairy is included in the protein category.)

✳ Encourage her to eat plenty of non-starchy vegetables as she would like, including broccoli, cauliflower, cabbage, green beans, asparagus, radishes, mushrooms, green leafy vegetables, cucumber, and celery. These vitamin- and fiber-rich vegetables contain very few calories and will fill her up.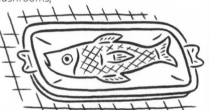

✳ Fat is the support substance for the human immune system, and it promotes mental function. Everyone needs to eat some fat in order to survive. Your partner may save on calories by selecting fat-containing foods that also are high in protein, including lean meats, fish, eggs, nuts, and seeds.

✳ If her sweet tooth beckons, visit your local health food store or pharmacy to stock up on a variety of 30-30-40 bars in chocolate, fruit, and other flavors.

✳ Suggest that she drink two full glasses of water before each meal, which will help control her appetite during that meal. She may want to add sea salt and honey to her water in order to make a natural "sports drink," giving her sodium and other minerals required by active and breastfeeding new mothers.

* If your partner finishes eating and indicates that she is still hungry, she may be more hungry for entertainment than for food. Encourage her to grab the baby and stroller and head out for a walk. Gently discourage her from reacting to her fatigue, sleeplessness, or boredom by taking a trip to the refrigerator!

When to Get More Help:

If, despite your partner's increased activity and regulated eating habits for several weeks, she is unable to shed her pregnancy weight, encourage her to contact her physician for a referral.

Exercise & Activity after Vaginal Delivery

The Facts:

General convention dictates that new mothers should restrict their activities for the first six weeks after delivery. However, as long as the new mother is feeling strong and well, the only activities that *must* be restricted are those requiring

- ⊙ balance

- ⊙ extreme stretches, such as the splits

- ⊙ unusual positions, such as those involved in some forms of yoga

What You Can Do:

* Perhaps the most important thing a new mother can do following her delivery is to begin to get back into her normal routine. Encourage her to gradually resume the activities she engaged in prior to her delivery, as long as they do not cause her discomfort.

* Help your partner introduce an exercise program into her daily schedule as early as possible. Even if she is only able to engage in light walking while pushing a stroller, encourage her to make time every day for getting out and exercising. After all, exercise can be an important time to think, plan, and help maintain one's sanity during a challenging time.

* Suggest that your partner inform her physician of her exercise program and activities and ask him or her to describe the symptoms that would necessitate a call to the doctor.

* Although traditionally abdominal exercises have been discouraged immediately after delivery, it is now recommended that

women begin or resume abdominal and Kegel exercises as soon as they feel comfortable doing so. Even the smoothest of deliveries may have caused trauma to the muscles of the vagina and pelvis. By doing gentle abdominal and Kegel exercises, your partner can help strengthen her vaginal muscles and prevent urinary leakage. For more information about Kegel exercises, see "Loss of Urinary or Vaginal Control" (page 155).

* If your partner sustained vaginal tearing or an episiotomy cut during delivery, remind her not to engage in any activities that might cause discomfort to the vaginal area. She should avoid activities like squatting and doing the splits until her perineum is completely healed.

* For restrictions on activity after C-section, see "Exercise & Activity after C-Section" (page 52).

When to Get More Help:

If your partner feels pain during any activity, suggest that she refrain from this activity temporarily and contact her physician.

Loss of Urinary or Vaginal Control

The Facts:

Today's babies are larger than the babies delivered by previous generations of women, for a variety of reasons. Eight- and nine-pound babies are becoming increasingly more common. Larger babies often mean that the tissue and muscle of a woman's vagina sustains more trauma during delivery—more stretching and tearing—and has a greater chance of requiring an episiotomy cut.

As a result, following delivery new mothers often experience uncontrolled urinary leakage when running or walking quickly, jumping, laughing, coughing, or sneezing. Their vaginal openings may not be as tight as they were before, and they may experience an eventual mild prolapse (falling) of the uterus and bladder or a protrusion of the rectum into the vaginal wall. These conditions lead new mothers to experience the following symptoms:

- diminished control of urination

- a feeling that their vaginal walls have lost their tightness, such that they do not feel their partner's sexual organ during intercourse

- a constant feeling of pressure, as if the bladder is pushing on the vagina

If a new mother experiences any of these symptoms, it is vital that she take steps to remedy these conditions. Loss of urinary control and inability to enjoy sexual intercourse do not need to be a part of motherhood.

What You Can Do:

PREVENTION:

❋ Encourage your partner to be active throughout her pregnancy.

The more mobile she is, the quicker her muscles will return to their previous shape and condition.

* Suggest that she learn how to perform Kegel exercises, a means of strengthening the vaginal and pelvic muscles. These exercises are useful for controlling urinary function and maintaining vaginal muscle tone. When she performs a Kegel exercise, she will slowly contract and then release her vaginal muscles as if she is trying to stop her flow of urine. These exercises should be repeated three to ten times a day, squeezing for ten seconds each time and repeating ten squeezes in a row. Some women make a habit of doing their Kegel exercises in the car while sitting at traffic lights or on the bus or train, ensuring that they become a part of their daily routine.

* Unless she is otherwise advised by her physician, encourage her to strengthen her abdominal muscles throughout her pregnancy. Pre-pregnancy abdominal workouts can be maintained until the fourteenth week of pregnancy. After this time, encourage her to perform upper abdominal exercises that do not crush the pregnant uterus between her chest and knees. Swimming is also an excellent low-impact back- and abdominal-strengthening exercise in any trimester.

TREATMENT:

* After delivery, suggest that she continue her Kegel exercises—a great way to tone the vaginal muscles and regain urinary and vaginal muscle control.

* To build and maintain vaginal and urinary control, encourage your partner to ensure that her vagina is well-lubricated prior to sexual intercourse. See "Low or No Vaginal Lubrication & Elasticity" (page 158) for more information.

* If your partner cannot control the leaking of urine following her delivery, using a combination estriol (a form of estrogen) and testosterone cream may help remedy the situation. Estriol

will help increase the elasticity of the vaginal and periurethral walls, while testosterone will help strengthen the muscle tissue that controls the flow of urine. To apply the cream, your partner will insert a quarter-size amount into the vagina and under the urethra. The cream should be applied behind and on either side of the area where she urinates, essentially the ten o'clock and two o'clock positions behind the urethra. This combination cream must be obtained from a compounding pharmacy (a pharmacy that formulates specialized medications, including natural hormone preparations) with a physician's prescription and is safe for use when breastfeeding. Too much testosterone creates symptoms such as oily skin, blemishes, and more aggressive behavior.

When to Get More Help:

If, after six weeks of doing regular Kegel exercises, your partner still experiences significant urinary leakage or lack of vaginal control, suggest that she seek the advice of her physician.

Low or No Vaginal Lubrication & Elasticity

The Facts:

While it may seem unrelated to delivering a baby, it is common for a new mother to experience an absence of vaginal lubrication and elasticity in the weeks and months following her delivery. Women who are not warned about this likelihood may believe that something is wrong, wondering if perhaps their obstetrician was too zealous in stitching up after delivery.

In fact, a lack of lubrication and elasticity is completely normal following delivery. Vaginal lubrication and elasticity are largely controlled by the estrogen hormone in a woman's body. After delivery, a new mother's estrogen goes from a very high level in late pregnancy to a *very* low level in the hours after the baby is born. This drop in estrogen affects the inner lining of the uterus, reducing vaginal elasticity and lubrication. For women (without vaginal tearing or episiotomy cuts) who resume their sexual activity in the first few weeks following delivery, dryness and lack of elasticity may cause discomfort during intercourse. Obviously, if a new mother attempts sexual activity too soon after her delivery, she will feel some pain and discomfort.

Lack of elasticity and lubrication will fade once your partner's body resumes its production of estrogen at its pre-pregnancy levels. Reaching pre-pregnancy estrogen level may take a few months or even a year, depending on how long your partner breastfeeds and how long it takes for her menstrual period to return.

After the tissues have healed from the birth, reduced lubrication and elasticity should not prevent a woman from resuming her sexual activity. In fact, the longer she waits, the more "tight" the vaginal opening will seem and the more uncomfortable initial sexual activity will be.

What You Can Do:

* Visit your local pharmacy for one of several over-the-counter glycerin-and-water-based lubricants, such as Astroglide and K-Y Jelly.

* Estrogen replacement is also an option. While vaginal lubricants help to synthetically replace the vaginal moisture usually produced by estrogen, estrogen replacement allows your partner to assist her body in reviving its own natural production of lubrication. Applying cream made with natural estriol—a mild form of estrogen that figures most prominently during pregnancy—changes the environment of the vagina from dry and nonelastic to moist and elastic within two weeks of use. Estriol cream and suppositories also help reestablish the "friendly bacteria" that protect the vagina from infection and will also protect her urinary system and bladder and urethra function.

   If your partner would like to try using estriol, encourage her to contact her physician for a prescription. She may use 1 to 2 milligrams of either the cream or the suppository form daily, inserted into the vagina. Estriol is safe for use when breastfeeding and may be used indefinitely, but most women cease using this product once their natural lubrication returns, within two to three months, or after six months if breastfeeding.

When to Get More Help:

If, after two weeks of using estriol cream, your partner's vagina still feels dry and painful, encourage her to seek the advice of her physician.

Constipation

The Facts:

New mothers experience constipation after delivery due to:

- immobility following delivery

- poor diet

- dehydration

- pain medications that contain narcotics

- reluctance to have a bowel movement for fear of episiotomy or rectal wound pain or re-tearing

What You Can Do:

* If your partner experienced constipation during her pregnancy,
encourage her to use whatever gentle remedies were helpful to
her in the past.

* Help her to keep hydrated by consuming eight to twelve
glasses of water a day. Place a pitcher of water at your partner's bedside and keep it filled with fresh water while she is
recovering. Bring her a tall glass of ice water whenever she is
breastfeeding the baby. New mothers should also avoid
caffeinated foods and beverages, since caffeine is a diuretic
that depletes the body of fluids.

* Suggest that she modify her
diet in order to avoid constipation. Serve her nutritious meals that include
fibrous, non-starchy fruits
and vegetables such as
figs, dates, prunes, broccoli,

asparagus, peas, and cabbage and fiber products from your local pharmacy.

* Assist your partner in increasing her activity level—the more she moves, the more her bowels will move. Invite her to tuck the baby into the stroller or sling and accompany you on walks, even if only around the neighborhood or to a shopping mall. Activity and exercise will benefit her body, by helping to alleviate constipation and assisting her body in the healing process, but it will also benefit her mind—by giving her an opportunity to spend time away from her usual routine and reflect on her new reality. She should reduce her activity level if she feels fatigued, dizzy, or otherwise uncomfortable.

! **Recognize that helping a new mother get back to her usual active lifestyle may entail taking over child-care duties or arranging for child care so that she can exercise (or simply catch up on sleep, since it is difficult to expend energy when one is sleep deprived). Be creative and generous in your assistance to her—as overwhelmed as you may be by your new role, she is likely to be more overwhelmed.**

* Magnesium is nature's constipation buster. Visit your local health food store for magnesium carbonate, magnesium oxide, or other form of magnesium that is *not* easily absorbed by the body. Encourage her to supplement her diet with 250 milligrams twice daily, slowly increasing her dosage every few days until her stool becomes soft. After the first week, she should try to cut down her dose so long as she maintains normal bowel movements.

* At the store, also look for glycerin suppositories and give them to your partner to use as directed.

* Visit your pharmacy for mild over-the-counter products that help alleviate constipation, including Metamucil and Fleet enema, to be used as directed and as needed.

! A new mother should not use suppositories or insert anything into her rectum if she sustained third- or fourth-
degree lacerations during her delivery. See "Caring for
Tears & Cuts" (page 30) for more information.

When to Get More Help:

If your partner is unable to have a bowel movement for more
than three days, or if she experiences constant, severe abdominal
cramping that she does not associate with breastfeeding, you or
she should contact her physician.

If a new mother experiences constipation for the first time
in the first three to four weeks after delivery, see "Thyroid
Disorder That Develops after Delivery" (page 91).

Changes in Her Abdominal Area

The Facts:

After the baby is born, a new mother's abdominal area appears significantly different from the way it looked before and during pregnancy. She will probably experience the following changes:

- Skin that had previously stretched to accommodate a full uterus now hangs loosely.

- Stretch marks that gradually developed and were faint when the skin was stretched tight in late pregnancy are now more obvious and appear red.

- The two abdominal muscles that previously met in the middle of her abdomen are now separated and have a space between them.

- The belly button may be "popped" out.

- A vertical line of pigment is visible from her belly button to her pubic bone.

What happened? During pregnancy, your partner's abdominal skin gradually stretched to accommodate several pounds of baby and pregnancy fluids. Once the baby and fluids leave the body, the skin and belly button don't snap back immediately. Additionally, during the second and third trimesters of pregnancy, your partner probably severely curtailed her abdominal exercise, resulting in abdominal muscles that have been relatively inactive for several months. And hormonal changes during pregnancy caused the line from her belly button to her pubic bone to darken.

The good news is that your partner's body will begin changing back to its former shape almost immediately. With time, nearly all of the excess skin around your partner's abdomen will contract and become more firm and tight, her belly button will pop back in, and the vertical line of pigment will fade.

What You Can Do:

* As with all other body changes associated with pregnancy and delivery, be as supportive as you've ever been. Be *more* supportive than you thought you could be. After all, she's likely to feel very sensitive about how her body looks after delivery—any comment other than a positive one may very well reinforce any harsh self-criticism she has already subjected herself to. Tell her she looks beautiful. Tell her you love her. Reassure her that Mother Nature will do her job in bringing her body back to its former shape.

* Skin requires hydration from the inside in order to snap back into shape and allow scars to fade. Encourage your partner to drink eight to twelve glasses of water per day. Help her stay hydrated by placing a pitcher of water at your partner's bedside and keeping it filled with fresh water while she is recovering. Bring her a tall glass of ice water whenever she is breastfeeding the baby.

* Stretch marks can also be encouraged to fade by hydrating the skin from the outside. Visit your local pharmacy, health food store, or department store for one of several stretch mark creams available. See "Stretch Marks" (page 166) for more information.

* If your partner is uncomfortable with the possibility of her "popped" belly button showing through form-fitting clothing, suggest that she place a small adhesive bandage over her belly button.

* If your partner is self-conscious about the line down her abdomen, suggest that she consult a dermatologist who can help cause this line to fade.

* Eating a healthy diet and getting enough exercise greatly help a new mother get back into shape. See "Ideal Postpartum Diet" (page 148) and "Exercise & Activity after Vaginal Delivery" (page 153) for more information.

When to Get More Help:

If, despite following the recommendations outlined above, your partner's body does not return to a condition that she is comfortable with, encourage her to contact her physician for a recommendation.

If your partner continues to feel uncomfortable about the discoloration of her abdominal line and area around the belly button, suggest that she contact a dermatologist for assistance in fading these darker areas.

Stretch Marks

The Facts:

Stretch marks are elongated marks on the skin caused by rapid stretching of the skin during late pregnancy. They commonly appear on the abdomen, thighs, and backside. Some new mothers get stretch marks more than others, for the following reasons:

- ⊙ genetic predisposition

- ⊙ predisposition to develop keloids (thick scarring)

- ⊙ lack of moisture in the skin

- ⊙ large baby or multiple babies

- ⊙ large amount of amniotic fluid

Toward the end of pregnancy, your partner's abdominal skin is stretched tightly, causing any marks to appear light in color. Once your baby and pregnancy fluids are delivered, your partner's skin snaps back like an accordion, causing the marks to appear darker, wider, and more pronounced. In some cases they take on a deep red color.

The good news is that, within six months following delivery, the majority of these marks will fade and become less pronounced. With time, nearly all of the excess skin around your partner's abdomen will contract and become more firm and tight.

What You Can Do:

TREATMENT:

- ✴ When skin is hydrated it is better able to stretch without becoming as severely marked. Encourage your partner to drink eight to twelve glasses of water daily during pregnancy.

- ✴ During and after pregnancy, moisturizing the areas most susceptible to marking—your partner's abdomen, thighs, and buttocks—is likely to reduce the development of marks. Visit your local health food store or pharmacy for one of a variety of moisturizing products. Because your partner's skin and body are particularly sensitive during pregnancy and after delivery, and because anything she applies to her skin will be passed to your baby, choose natural products with simple ingredients, including olive oil, vitamin E, and royal bee jelly. If the ingredient names are long and hard to pronounce, the product may not be as "pure" as you would like it to be. Ideally, moisturizers should be absorbed easily by the skin and leave it feeling soft. Encourage your partner to massage moisturizer into her abdomen, thighs, and buttocks every morning after her shower and every evening before bed.

* Once your baby is born, your partner's body will require more water than ever—particularly if she is breastfeeding. Some of that water will be used to hydrate her skin and help any stretch marks fade. Encourage your partner to drink at least eight to twelve glasses of water daily.

* If your partner would like to further increase the elasticity of her skin and help her stretch marks fade, suggest that she ask her physician about obtaining a cream containing estriol, a mild form of estrogen that increases the elasticity of the skin. Estriol is available from a compounding pharmacy (a pharmacy that formulates specialized medications, including natural hormone preparations) and requires a prescription. Estriol is safe for use when breastfeeding.

* Visit your local health food store for natural supplements that will help your partner's body heal as quickly as possible. Antioxidants such as vitamin C, vitamin E, alpha lipoic acid, and co-enzyme Q10 can be very helpful and should be used as directed. Suggest that your partner check with her physician to make sure that the supplements she takes are safe for use when breastfeeding.

* Perhaps the most important thing you can do is to maintain a positive attitude about her stretch marks. Remember that, however concerned you are about her appearance, she is more concerned. What was a glorious pregnant abdomen suddenly looks like a not-so-glorious "beer gut" streaked with stretch marks. She knows this. Remarking about the unappealing appearance of her stretch marks will only make her feel worse. If she asks, tell her that you love her, that you love your baby, and that she is beautiful.

When to Get More Help:

If your partner's stretch marks have not faded to her satisfaction six months following delivery, assist her in arranging to see a dermatologist for additional recommendations.

Hair Loss

The Facts:

Beginning about three months after delivery, many women experience some thinning of the hair on their heads due to:

- a rapid drop in estrogen level after delivery

- an increase in testosterone, the male hormone associated with male pattern baldness, after delivery

- a deficiency of progesterone, a female hormone that generally blocks the conversion of normal testosterone to dihydrotestosterone (DHT), the form of testosterone associated with male pattern baldness

- a deficiency of the thyroid hormone

- a deficiency of iron, related to loss of blood after delivery

- dehydration, poor nutrition, and stress following the delivery

The good news is that new mothers who lose hair after delivery—even a large quantity of hair—can expect their hair to grow back within three to six months.

? Does hair loss following a delivery result in women going bald, as with male pattern baldness? No. Most women report an overall thinning of their head hair, such that their hair feels less full. It is common for the new mother to be the only person who notices this change.

What You Can Do:

* Encourage her to watch her diet. The quality and quantity of hair, nails, and anything else produced by her body are largely

dependent on what she puts into her body. Encourage her to eat simple, nutrient-rich foods and avoid processed junk food. This will ensure that the building blocks for her new hair production are as strong as they should be. See "Ideal Postpartum Diet" (page 148) for more information.

* Stress and anxiety have a powerful effect on the body. When we simply recognize and try to resolve the sources of our stress, our bodies are able to get back to their regular tasks, which include producing healthy hair, nails, energy, and so on. Your partner is tackling many new responsibilities and may feel overwhelmed. Simply talking about these trials may help her to gain a sense of control over them. Assist her in getting whatever help she needs. See chapter 9, "Resuming Your Life Together," for specific suggestions on how to help your partner resolve problems associated with her new balancing act.

* The human body requires an ample supply of water to function at an optimal level. Encourage your partner to drink eight to twelve glasses of water daily.

* Often an iron deficiency can result in hair loss or slow hair regrowth. If your partner expresses concern about her hair loss (and only if *she* expresses concern), suggest that she contact her physician in order to determine whether her blood is iron deficient.

* An underproductive thyroid gland can also result in hair loss or slow hair regrowth. Suggest that when she visits her physician to determine whether her blood is iron deficient, she also request a blood test to determine how much thyroid her body is producing. Blood tests of this type should check the T3 Free, T4 Free, and TSH levels, as other tests may be less accurate. If your partner is losing her hair and is told that her thyroid level is at the low end of normal, or just on the line between low and normal, encourage her to ask for medication to boost her thyroid level anyway. Make sure any supplements she is given are *natural* thyroid products.

* In some cases, an overproduction of testosterone caused by an estrogen deficiency can cause head hair loss. If your partner begins to experience oily skin and acne breakouts and becomes more impatient, her body may be overproducing testosterone. By taking a natural estrogen supplement, your partner can help her body to combat the excessive testosterone. The body does this by producing a hormone called sex-binding globulin, which binds to and controls the excessive testosterone. Suggest that she contact her physician for more information.

* Most important, never disregard her complaints regarding hair thinning and loss. Imagine how traumatic hair loss would be for you; consider how much more traumatic it is for her. If she confides in you about her concerns, listen patiently, tell her that she is beautiful, and make suggestions based on those outlined above. Because she may be too busy in her new role to research these solutions, offer to help her find health-care providers who might be able to treat her hair loss.

When to Get More Help:

If your partner's physician indicates that he or she is not familiar with the remedies mentioned above or their ability to help correct hair loss, help your partner find a gynecologist with training in natural hormone replacement therapy, a board-certified physician specializing in "anti-aging" and hormones, or a dermatologist specializing in hair loss. Also, recognize that despite prevention efforts, losing hair after delivery is a natural result of postpartum hormonal changes and may not be avoided in many cases. The prevention options provided here may lessen hair loss in those women whose amount of hair loss is not related to these changes. Most women will regain the majority of the hair they lose in the months that follow delivery.

The New Mother's
Mind

Recognizing,
Preventing & Treating
Postpartum Depression
& Mood Changes

7

AN OVERVIEW OF POSTPARTUM DEPRESSION

M ost new mothers experience some mood changes in the weeks or months after their baby is born. This chapter provides basic information on postpartum depression—its causes, symptoms, and treatment methods.

What Is Postpartum Depression?

Postpartum depression can be defined as mild, significant, or severe mood changes and depression that arise in mothers following the birth of a baby. Often the symptoms seem to come out of nowhere—all of a sudden, a usually well-adjusted woman becomes severely depressed; is unable to get out of bed and function normally; is unable to sleep; feels agitated or panicky; and has obsessive thoughts, feelings of hopelessness, crying spells, and abrupt changes in mood and energy level.

If left untreated, postpartum mood changes may become worse with time. Some women experience increasingly strong thoughts of suicide and begin to fear harming their babies.

What Is It Like to Have Postpartum Depression?

Many men have a difficult time understanding how their partner with postpartum depression feels. To get a sense of how bewildering and scary it can be to have postpartum depression, imagine yourself finally getting a shot at the job of your dreams. On your first day of work, the boss walks into your spacious office and extends a welcoming hand. Suddenly, you feel a surge of anger and, in an uncontrollable spasm, you reach out your hand and slap him across the face! Wow! Where did that come from? you wonder. But before you can fully appreciate the absurdity of your actions, you feel a wave of sadness and hopelessness. You open your mouth to speak, and you find yourself telling the boss that you're not worthy of this job and that he would have fired you anyway. You stomp out of the office, slamming the door behind you, and slump down to the floor in a fit of tears.

The scenario above, while somewhat exaggerated, gives you some idea of how a woman suffering from postpartum mood changes feels. She doesn't understand her sudden emotional surges, her actions, or the words coming out of her mouth, yet she can't seem to stop her mouth and body. Despite what she says and does, the real woman you chose to spend your life with is still somewhere inside, horrified at her words and actions, wishing she could make it all go away and feeling just as confused and frustrated as you are.

Interestingly, because postpartum mood changes follow a happy, highly anticipated time in a couple's life together—namely, the birth of a baby—it is often difficult for a new father to understand and recognize his partner's seemingly nonsensical reaction. For this reason, the diagnosis and treatment of postpartum mood changes are often delayed unnecessarily.

When new mothers do seek treatment, many are told that they should ignore the problem and that it will fade. Often, it's only when postpartum mood changes become extremely pronounced that they receive attention. Luckily, this approach is becoming less common as doctors, patients, and family become more informed about the seriousness of the problem and the tragedy that may result if it is left untreated.

The Three Levels of Postpartum Mood Changes

"BABY BLUES"

Approximately 80 percent of new mothers experience mild, tolerable intermittent "blues" or mood swings, discussed in "Mild Mood Swings, Including Mild Anxiety & Depression" (page 81). Baby blues often begin in the first three days after delivery and fade within two to six weeks.

POSTPARTUM DEPRESSION

Approximately 15 percent of new mothers suffer from actual postpartum depression. What begins as baby blues may slowly become more severe, until the new mother's behavior is dominated by the characteristics of one or more of the three types of postpartum depression:

- ⊙ depression

- ⊙ anxiety and agitation

- ⊙ obsessive-compulsive behavior

POSTPARTUM PSYCHOSIS

Less than 1 percent of new mothers suffer from an extreme version of postpartum mood changes called postpartum psychosis, in which the new mother is unable to maintain a hold on reality. It is common for a woman with postpartum psychosis to hallucinate—seeing things and hearing voices that aren't there—and act in such a way that she presents a danger to herself, her partner, her new baby, and her other children. This condition is rare but very serious and requires immediate hospitalization and psychiatric treatment. Postpartum psychosis can develop within the first few days or weeks following delivery and as late as one year after delivery. The psychosis related to this condition can be brought under control by professional mental health treatment within two to six weeks.

Postpartum depression and postpartum psychosis are serious medical conditions, and a new mother suffering from one of these conditions deserves the attention, patience, and sympathy that you would provide to any ill person. Baby blues, while not as dangerous as postpartum depression and postpartum psychosis, is also a serious condition that requires attention, especially since it can develop into postpartum depression.

Why Do Postpartum Mood Changes Occur?

While most people think that hormonal changes are solely to blame for postpartum mood changes, many other circumstances can also contribute to their development. Below are the main contributing factors.

HORMONAL CHANGES AFTER DELIVERY

In the first hour after delivery, a new mother's levels of estrogen, progesterone, and other hormones go from very high to very low. These changes have a dramatic effect on her mood and psychological well-being.

In recent years, a better understanding of the use of natural estrogen and progesterone supplements has made a tremendous difference in the lives of countless new mothers. Many of the remedies described in this guidebook focus on this quick, drug-free, and side-effect-free method.

SLEEP DEPRIVATION

A new mother's lack of sleep is a central contributing factor of postpartum mood changes. See "Sleep Deprivation & Insomnia" (page 76) and "A Parent's Guide to Adjusting to New Sleep Patterns" (page 228) for more information.

ADRENAL OVERSTIMULATION AND EXHAUSTION

Childbirth is an exciting and stressful time that often causes a rise in a new mother's adrenal hormones—cortisol, adrenaline, pregnenolone, and other hormones designed to provide humans with bursts of energy during times of crisis. As the baby gets older, the challenges associated with the mother's new role increase rather than diminish. If the new mother does not get the rest she needs, her adrenal gland will continue to pump out these "fight or flight" hormones until it becomes exhausted. This is particularly true for new mothers who try to be "super moms," refusing assistance from friends, family members, and others around them. Adrenal exhaustion can contribute to postpartum mood changes.

OVERWHELMING FEELINGS ASSOCIATED WITH NEW RESPONSIBILITIES OF MOTHERHOOD

The moment a woman sees her baby in the delivery room, she is keenly aware that she is now responsible for a whole other person besides herself. Moreover, once she brings her baby home, she may be further overwhelmed by the difference between the fantasy of new motherhood and the far more difficult reality.

OVERWHELMING FEELINGS ASSOCIATED WITH LACK OF SUPPORT

In the past, men and women did not raise their children in isolation. New mothers could expect to enjoy the assistance of a large extended family, who helped to educate the new mother and share the heavy responsibilities associated with caring for a newborn. Today, many women become overwhelmed when they bring a baby home from the hospital to find that they have no help— and no instruction manual—for this little person who seems to require more time and energy than her healing body can provide.

LONELINESS AND ISOLATION

Because many women must tackle the challenges of new motherhood without the help of an extended family, the first few days and weeks of motherhood are often spent in relative seclusion. As a result, many women begin to develop feelings of loneliness and isolation from the outside world. These feelings often contribute indirectly to postpartum mood changes. Moreover, if a new mother begins having inappropriate thoughts (such as obsessive-compulsive thoughts associated with one type of postpartum depression), she is likely to isolate herself even further.

OTHER RISK FACTORS

Finally, some new mothers are predisposed to developing postpartum depression. This predisposition may be related to a history of physical or sexual abuse in childhood, a history of severe premenstrual syndrome (PMS), or a history of mood changes associated with taking oral contraceptives.

How Postpartum Mood Changes Are Treated

Commonly, new mothers and fathers searching for solutions to postpartum mood changes find the following approaches to treatment.

PHARMACEUTICAL SOLUTIONS

It is common for health-care professionals to prescribe antidepressant medication to women whose moods do not elevate after a short time or sleeping pills to women who cannot sleep. Although antidepressant medication may elevate the mother's mood while she takes it, and sleeping pills may help her sleep, they do not address the underlying causes of these problems. Additionally, taking these medications may require a new mother to stop breastfeeding, which may cause her to feel further alienated from her baby. Finally, the stigma that many women associate with taking prescription medication may cause a new mother to delay getting treatment in the first place, thereby causing her symptoms to become more pronounced and harder to treat. However, especially in the case of postpartum psychosis, antidepressants can sometimes have long-term benefits when used for a short time in conjunction with psychotherapy and nutritional and hormonal treatments.

SELF-HELP GROUPS

Many women who have gone through postpartum mood changes have taken the initiative to create local, national, and on-line self-help groups that inform new mothers about these conditions and share tips and remedies for a variety of new-baby-related challenges. Participating in these groups can be invaluable, especially when combined with other efforts to address the underlying nutritional and hormonal causes of post-partum mood change.

PSYCHOTHERAPY

Talk therapy can help a woman examine events or patterns in her past that affect how she sees herself as a mother, thereby helping her understand and manage her emotions related to new motherhood. Unfortunately, psychotherapy requires time, the very thing most new mothers lack. Moreover, the stigma that some women associate with seeking help may cause a new mother to avoid this type of treatment, thereby causing her symptoms to worsen. However, individual therapy or group therapy can be helpful when combined with a program that addresses the nutritional, hormonal, and baby-related factors that contribute to postpartum mood changes.

The Approach of This Guidebook

The severity of a woman's postpartum mood change will depend on how quickly it is identified and how promptly it is treated. While traditional treatment methods may take six months to one year to become effective, the "early detection approach" and the remedies suggested in this guidebook can help new mothers and fathers resolve the majority of symptoms within a few weeks to six months, depending on the acuteness of the symptoms.

You will find that this guidebook directly addresses the physiological, emotional, and logistical issues related to postpartum mood changes. This guidebook also provides concrete tools to help prevent, identify, manage, and quickly treat postpartum mood changes and prevent the recurrence of this condition in future pregnancies. All of the suggested recommendations are intended to be easy to implement and provide the new father with ways to make things easier for his partner, thereby strengthening the family bonds during this challenging time.

8
SOLUTIONS
FOR POSTPARTUM
DEPRESSION

Mild Postpartum Depression or "Baby Blues"

The Facts:

Although statistics indicate that more than 80 percent of new mothers experience some form of postpartum mood change, including "baby blues," not all of these mood changes require serious treatment. *Some* confusion, fear, and introspection is entirely appropriate in light of the new responsibilities and dramatic changes in lifestyle that come with a new baby. Mild postpartum depression generally passes within two weeks.

Although extensive treatment is not necessary for mild cases, it is important to take all mood changes seriously. Taking notice immediately and making small adjustments can prevent the development of more serious postpartum depression at best and immediately improve the lifestyle of the new father and mother at worst.

Symptoms of mild postpartum depression or baby blues include:

- unhappiness regarding new motherhood

- episodes of crying

- quiet, less expressive moods

- behavior that is more reclusive than usual

- a greater tendency to complain or vocalize criticism

What You Can Do:

- Talk with your partner immediately if she exhibits any of the symptoms listed above. Open the line of communication between you. Acknowledge her unhappiness. Ask her to express her sadness or frustration—*every* time she feels this

way. You may find that her introspection relates to a feeling of "failure" for having had a C-section when she wanted to deliver vaginally. She may believe you wanted a boy when she delivered a girl. She may be horrified by the appearance of her body after the delivery. Or she may be overwhelmed by the huge amount of work required to care for the baby and may be having trouble getting organized. Take this opportunity to comfort her and find solutions together.

* Don't tell her that "everything will be OK."

* Don't cause her to feel that her attitude is "spoiling" her time as a new mother. Although it may be true, your partner cannot help her feelings, and your comments are only likely to make her feel worse.

* Don't expect her to hide her unhappiness around friends and family members. Keep in mind that she cannot control these mood changes any more than she would be able to control a broken leg. Shaming her will only exacerbate her condition. See "What Is It Like to Have Postpartum Depression?" (page 174) for more information.

* Regardless of the severity of her symptoms, encourage your partner to speak to her physician or other health-care profes- sional about her baby blues and keep him or her updated every

few days. If your partner is unable or unwilling to do this, take the initiative yourself.

❋ For more information on treating baby blues nutritionally, see "Mild Mood Swings, Including Mild Anxiety & Depression" (page 81).

When to Get More Help:

If you notice that your partner's baby blues seem to be worsening, even slightly, review the recommendations offered in "Postpartum Depression (Dominated by Depression)" (page 185) and encourage her to contact her physician for additional assistance. If she does not call her physician, take the initiative on her behalf.

Postpartum Depression (Dominated by Depression)

The Facts:

Postpartum depression comes in three different forms:

- postpartum depression dominated by feelings of depression

- postpartum depression dominated by feelings of anxiety and panic

- postpartum depression dominated by obsessive-compulsive feelings

Most women experience some combination of the conditions described above.

Postpartum depression dominated by depression is essentially a more pronounced version of baby blues, characterized by the following symptoms:

- a tendency to be quiet or withdrawn

- an inability to sleep or a tendency to oversleep

- mild memory lapses or significant forgetfulness

- an increase or decrease in appetite

- crying spells or hysteria

- complaints that grow to be unrealistic

- uncharacteristic activities or loss of interest in favorite activities

- loss of interest or excessive interest in her personal hygiene

- a tendency to be uncommunicative or evasive

- a tendency to become stressed and overwhelmed very quickly

- a tendency to exhibit feelings of shame, fear, or incompetence

- no expression of relief when reassured

- worsening of the foregoing symptoms

The symptoms of this type of postpartum depression can start off mild, slowly becoming more serious, until the new mother begins entertaining thoughts of suicide or of harming the baby or her other children.

If postpartum depression is addressed early, it can be treated without medication but with lifestyle and nutritional changes instead. While the list of suggestions below is long, keep in mind that any steps you take will assist your partner in her recovery.

What You Can Do:

LIFESTYLE CHANGES:

* First and foremost, recognize that your partner's mood changes are not voluntary. Postpartum depression is an unfortunate consequence of recovering from pregnancy and childbirth. She is experiencing an illness and requires your care and support. For more information, see "What Is It Like to Have Postpartum Depression?" (page 174).

* Open the line of communication between you. Postpartum depression is often characterized by feelings of loneliness, alienation, shame, and failure. Simply talking about these feelings is likely to help her feel better. Be kind; be patient; be encouraging. Tell her that you regard her as the most courageous woman you know. If you believe that you cannot be as available as you would like to be, arrange for her to speak to someone else—a friend, a family member, or a professional— who can regularly encourage her to speak about her feelings.

Checking in with her regularly will also enable you to keep tabs on her mental state so that you can get additional help for her if her symptoms worsen.

✳ Make a plan to treat the whole woman—her mind (e.g., her emotional concerns), her body (e.g., her diet), and her lifestyle (e.g, the logistics associated with bringing home a new baby). All of these aspects of her life must be addressed simultaneously in order for her to feel that she is regaining control of her life.

✳ Assist your partner in getting more sleep. Sleep deprivation is a *major* contributor to feelings of depression—perhaps the most significant cause second to hormonal deficiencies. See "Sleep Deprivation & Insomnia" (page 76) and "A Parent's Guide to Adjusting to New Sleep Patterns" (page 228) for more information.

✳ Help your partner evaluate the many new responsibilities associated with having a baby. In earlier times, family members and friends would provide active assistance to new parents in the first few weeks, months, and years of a child's life, giving the mother support so that she could focus on recovering from childbirth and learning to care for her baby. Today, many couples live far from family and friends, and women wind up learning how to care for a baby on their own while healing from the delivery. Even if you are fortunate enough to have a support network on which to rely, help her determine how she will find time to sleep, exercise, eat properly, and spend time with friends. Provide as much assistance around the house as you can. See chapter 9, "Resuming Your Life Together," in this guidebook for more information.

✳ Eating simple, nutritious foods goes a long way toward helping the body and mind heal. When a body needn't expend extra energy processing the artificial colors, flavors, and chemicals in junk food, it can better perform the jobs of resting, repairing, and maintaining proper mental function. Encourage your partner to maintain a healthful diet and avoid processed foods. For more information on how you can help your partner eat well, see "Ideal Postpartum Diet" (page 148).

* Dehydration is a key culprit in depression. Encourage your partner to stay hydrated by drinking at least eight to twelve glasses of water daily, and even more if she is breastfeeding. Drinking water will help your partner's body cleanse itself of the medications and other substances given during and after labor that can strongly affect mood and mental focus. Also encourage her to take hot baths and saunas. See "Maintaining Hydration" (page 123) for more information.

* Another effective means of cleansing her system is the consumption of diuretic foods. Encourage her to eat asparagus, cucumber, and parsley and drink tea made of dandelion infusion.

MEDICAL TESTING:

* Diet and proper nutrition have a great influence on a new mother's mood and sense of well-being. Besides watching what she eats, one way for the new mother to monitor whether she is eating well enough is to test her insulin level. Encourage her to visit her physician in order to check her fasting insulin level. If her insulin level is under 5, it is possible that your partner is not eating enough food in general or carbohydrates in particular.

* Suggest that she ask her physician to test her DHEAS level. This hormone plays an important role in maintaining women's hormonal balance, functioning as a strong antidepressant that also promotes stamina and strength. If your partner's DHEAS

level is below 100, she is likely to benefit from supplementing this hormone. Ideally, she should begin by taking a 5-milligram pill per day and increase this dosage by 5 milligrams every two weeks, not exceeding 25 milligrams daily. Your partner should cut back her dosage if she begins to feel edgy or if her skin develops blemishes. DHEA is safe for use when breastfeeding.

* Also encourage her to have her blood tested for the following:

  ⊙ electrolyte and CO_2 levels (check electrolyte balance and pH balance; see "Maintaining Hydration," page 123, for more information)

  ⊙ thyroid function (see "Preexisting Thyroid Disorder," page 88, and "Thyroid Disorder That Develops after Delivery," page 91, for more information)

  ⊙ iron (to ensure that she is not anemic)

* Measuring your partner's cholesterol level is also a great idea. When her cholesterol level is too low, below 160, her mood and mental focus are significantly affected, making her more prone to depression. If your partner's cholesterol level is low, encourage her to take an amino acid called inositol—6,000 milligrams twice daily, not exceeding 12,000 milligrams daily. Inositol is safe for use when breastfeeding.

SUPPLEMENTS:

* During pregnancy, a woman's body maintains an extremely high level of the hormone progesterone. Within hours after delivery, her progesterone level drops far below its pre-pregnancy level. This progesterone deficiency is often the reason women become depressed after delivery. A simple injection of liquid progesterone (in oil) can result in a dramatic turnaround in mood within twelve to twenty-four hours. Approximately 50 percent of new mothers feel better the day after their first injection.

Progesterone of this type may be purchased at a compounding pharmacy (a pharmacy that formulates specialized medications, including natural hormone preparations) and requires a prescription from her physician. Her initial dose should be 200 to 300 milligrams, depending on the severity of her mood, followed by progesterone capsules or sublingual (under the tongue) drops the following day. If she takes capsules, encourage her to take 50 to 100 milligrams every four to six hours as needed. If her dosage is too high, she is likely to feel dizzy or sleepy, warranting a change in dosage. Sublingual progesterone drops may be used in similar doses; progesterone cream does not yield the same results. In postpartum depression, most women require another dose of injected liquid progesterone every five to ten days for two to six weeks. Progesterone therapy should continue from six weeks to six months, as needed. Progesterone injections, capsules, and sublingual drops are safe for use when breastfeeding. See "Anxiety & Irritability Due to Progesterone Deficiency" (page 102) for more information.

* During pregnancy, a woman's body maintains an extremely high level of the hormone estrogen. Within hours after delivery, your partner's estrogen level drops far below its pre-pregnancy level. This estrogen deficiency is often the reason women become depressed after delivery. Why does this occur? When estrogen levels goes down, the level of monoamine oxidase (MAO) goes up, decreasing the production of hormones that promote a sense of well-being. The result is depression. Replacing estrogen in order to promote the production of these hormones becomes more important when postpartum depression comes on gradually (i.e., after the first week or two).

If your partner's symptoms have set in gradually, using a natural estrogen supplement may help her. The earlier she begins estrogen therapy, the quicker her body's response will be. Encourage her to speak to her physician about supplementing estrogen in gel form, available by prescription from a compounding pharmacy; Triest (one gram of Triest gel is a combination of E1 [0.25 mg], E2 [0.75 mg], and E3 [2.5 mg]) is the recommended estrogen gel. She should rub 0.25 to 2 grams of Triest on her inner arm or inner thigh twice daily. If she uses too much, she will retain water and become edgy, nervous, or agitated. Natural estrogen is safe for use when breastfeeding, although it may slightly reduce her milk supply.

Women who are not able to obtain Triest gel from a compounding pharmacy may obtain a prescription for an E2 patch, but they may find that it is not as strong and therefore less helpful. One E2 patch is the Vivelle Dot, which in .05 mg or 0.1 mg dosages may be worn for three days at a time. Some women are able to wear three 0.1 Vivelle Dots without side effects. Alternatively, Triest (a combination of E1, E2, and E3) in sublingual (under the tongue) drop form may be used.

Within a few days, your partner will find that her estrogen supplement helps her sleep, concentrate, be more productive, have a greater interest in her body image, and generally feel happier. However, if her estrogen supplement doesn't seem to affect her, suggest that she try it again a few weeks later. Six weeks after beginning her estrogen therapy, suggest that she visit her physician in order to check the levels of estrogen in her blood. This test must be done six hours after her last dose. Recent medical studies confirm the effectiveness of estrogen treatment.

* The vitamin B family of supplements helps to improve mood and fight depression. Suggest that your partner take 1 milligram of vitamin B_{12} in sublingual (under the tongue) drops daily and 50 to 100 mg of a B-complex vitamin.

* 5-hydroxytryptophan is a substance derived from naturally occurring amino acids. It helps build levels of serotonin, the "happy hormone" that fights depression, compulsive behavior,

and anxiety. While many of the latest pharmaceutical antidepressant medications increase serotonin artificially, 5-hydroxytryptophan does this naturally, improving sleep in the process. You can obtain this natural supplement over the counter. Suggest that your partner begin taking 100 milligrams in the morning with breakfast, another 100 milligrams with lunch, and 200 milligrams at night without food. If she does not sense a significant improvement after ten days, suggest that she increase her morning and midday doses to 200 mg each and her evening dosage to 300. She should decrease her dosages if she begins feeling sleepy during the day or experiences diarrhea. 5-hydroxytryptophan is safe for use when breastfeeding but *should not be used by women who take other antidepressant medication in the SSRI category, such as Zoloft, Prozac, and Selexa.*

* St. John's wort is another natural supplement that helps to elevate mood. Visit your local health food store for St. John's wort in .3 percent extract form. Suggest that your partner take 300 milliliters three times daily. *This remedy is not appropriate for new mothers who use an antidepressant medication in the SSRI category, such as Zoloft, Prozac, and Selexa.* St. John's wort is safe for use when breastfeeding.

* S-adenosylmethionine (SAMe) is a natural supplement that helps to quickly alleviate a variety of depressive moods, in addition to cleansing the liver and promoting physical healing. SAMe is available at your local health food store. Suggest that your partner take 200 milligrams twice daily on an empty stomach—one in the morning and another before the sun sets. She can increase the dosage every other day, not to exceed 800 milligrams per dose and no more than 1600 mg per day. She should reduce her dose if she feels sleepy, edgy, or fuzzy headed. SAMe is safe for use when breastfeeding.

When to Get More Help:

Supplementing progesterone and estrogen requires a physician's prescription and a blood test to determine what her initial or "baseline" levels of these hormones are.

If the recommendations outlined above are not helpful, contact her physician for additional assistance. Don't hesitate to seek the support of family, friends, and organizations that assist families with postpartum depression.

Postpartum Depression (Dominated by Anxiety & Panic)

The Facts:

Postpartum depression comes in three different forms:

- ⊙ postpartum depression dominated by feelings of depression

- ⊙ postpartum depression dominated by feelings of anxiety and panic

- ⊙ postpartum depression dominated by obsessive-compulsive feelings

Most women experience some combination of the conditions described above.

Women suffering from postpartum depression that is dominated by episodes of severe anxiety and panic may experience the following symptoms in addition to the standard symptoms of depression:

- ⊙ intense feelings of fear

- ⊙ heart palpitations

- ⊙ heartbeat that is so rapid as to cause fear of a heart attack

- ⊙ hyperventilation

- ⊙ chest pains and indigestion

- ⊙ numbing or tingling sensation in their hands and feet

Postpartum depression of this type may be managed with proper care within a few weeks, as long as it is addressed promptly. New mothers who do not receive treatment for their condition commonly report the same symptoms with little or no improvement at four, six, and eight months after delivery. When treatment is delayed, women do not respond as well to natural methods and often require medication in order to treat the condition.

! The symptoms of the three types of postpartum depression often overlap. Many women suffer from postpartum depression that includes symptoms of all three types. Once you and your partner identify what her symptoms are, simply incorporate the remedies suggested for those symptoms in the corresponding section.

What You Can Do:

LIFESTYLE CHANGES:

* First and foremost, recognize that your partner's mood changes are not voluntary. Postpartum depression is an unfortunate consequence of recovering from pregnancy and childbirth. She is experiencing an illness and requires your care and support. For more information, see "What Is It Like to Have Postpartum Depression?" (page 174).

* Open the line of communication between you. Postpartum depression is often characterized by feelings of loneliness, alienation, shame, and failure. Simply talking about these feelings is likely to help her feel better. Be kind; be patient; be encouraging. Tell her that you regard her as the most courageous woman you know. If you believe that you cannot be as available as you would like to be, arrange for her to speak to someone else—a friend, a family member, or a professional—who can regularly encourage her to speak about her feelings. Checking in with her regularly will also enable you to keep tabs on her mental state so that you can get additional help for her if her symptoms worsen.

* Make a plan to treat the whole woman—her mind (e.g., her emotional concerns), her body (e.g., her diet), and her spirit lifestyle (e.g, the logistics associated with bringing home a new

baby). All of these aspects of her life must be addressed simultaneously in order for her to feel that she is regaining control of her life.

* If your partner's panic attacks cause her to fear that she is having a heart attack, help her to analyze the situation by using the following technique:

   Speak to her about her panic attacks. Ask her to alert you when she experiences her next attack. When she indicates that her heart is racing, gently hold her wrist in order to feel her pulse. Count her pulse beats for sixty seconds in order to determine her heart rate. Let her know what her heart rate is. It will probably go no higher than 90 or 100 beats per minute, which is not dangerous and not nearly high enough for cardiac arrest. In fact, just a few minutes into an ordinary aerobic workout, the heart rate may rise to 150!

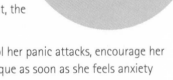

* To help your partner control her panic attacks, encourage her to use the following technique as soon as she feels anxiety coming on:

   1. Sit up straight, breathe in slowly, hold your breath for a few seconds, and exhale.

   2. Focus on the word "relax" and recall a restful vacation spot. Continue to breathe slowly until the anxiety passes.

* If your partner is anxious, it is likely that her body is producing a high amount of adrenaline, which produces a "fight or flight" response originally intended to help humans flee from natural predators. Overproduction of adrenaline can sometimes be triggered by a poor or unbalanced diet. To help your partner prevent a further rise of her adrenaline level, encourage her to

eat three nutritious meals and two snacks daily. Discourage her from adopting an all-carbohydrate or all-protein diet. A diet that balances intake of proteins, fats, and carbohydrates, such as The Zone, is ideal.

* Assist your partner in getting more sleep. Sleep deprivation is a *major* contributor to feelings of depression—perhaps the most significant cause second to hormonal deficiencies. See "Sleep Deprivation & Insomnia" (page 76) and "A Parent's Guide to Adjusting to New Sleep Patterns" (page 228) for more information.

* Help your partner evaluate the many new responsibilities associated with having a baby. In earlier times, family members and friends would provide active assistance to new parents in the first few weeks, months, and years of a child's life, giving the mother support so that she could focus on recovering from childbirth and learning to care for her baby. Today, many couples live far from family and friends, and women wind up learning how to care for a baby on their own while healing from the delivery. Even if you are fortunate enough to have a support network on which to rely, help her determine how she will find time to sleep, exercise, eat properly, and spend time with friends. Provide as much assistance around the house as you can. See chapter 9, "Resuming Your Life Together," in this guidebook for more information.

* Eating simple, nutritious foods goes a long way toward helping the body and mind heal. When a body needn't expend extra energy processing the artificial colors, flavors, and chemicals in junk food, it can better perform the jobs of resting, repairing, and maintaining proper mental function. Encourage your partner to maintain a healthful diet and avoid processed foods. For more information on how you can help your partner eat well, see "Ideal Postpartum Diet" (page 148).

* Dehydration is a key culprit in depression. Encourage your partner to stay hydrated by drinking at least eight to twelve glasses of water daily, and even more if she is breastfeeding. Drinking water will help your partner's body cleanse itself of the medications and other substances given during and after labor that can strongly affect mood and mental focus. Also encourage her to take hot baths and saunas. See "Maintaining Hydration" (page 123) for more information.

* Another effective means of cleansing her system is the consumption of diuretic foods. Encourage her to eat asparagus, cucumber, and parsley and drink tea made of dandelion infusion.

MEDICAL TESTING:

* Diet and proper nutrition have a great influence on a new mother's mood and sense of well-being. Besides watching what she eats, one way for the new mother to monitor whether she is eating well enough is to test her insulin level. Encourage her to visit her physician in order to check her fasting insulin level. If her insulin level is under 5, it is possible that your partner is not eating enough food in general or carbohydrates in particular.

* Suggest that she ask her physician to test her DHEAS level. This hormone plays an important role in maintaining women's hormonal balance, functioning as a strong antidepressant that also promotes stamina and strength. If your partner's DHEAS level is below 100, she is likely to benefit from supplementing this hormone. Ideally, she should begin by taking a 5-milligram pill per day and increase this dosage by 5 milligrams every two weeks, not exceeding 25 milligrams daily. Your partner should cut back her dosage if she begins to feel edgy or if her skin develops blemishes. DHEA is safe for use when breastfeeding.

* Also encourage her to have her blood tested for the following:

  ⊙ electrolyte and CO_2 levels (check electrolyte balance and pH balance; see "Maintaining Hydration," page 123, for more information)

  ⊙ thyroid function (see "Preexisting Thyroid Disorder," page 88, and "Thyroid Disorder That Develops after Delivery," page 91, for more information)

  ⊙ iron (to ensure that she is not anemic)

SUPPLEMENTS:

* Magnesium supplements are incredibly effective for calming anxiety. Visit your local health food store for fast-absorbing magnesium, such as magnesium glycinate, magnesium gluconate, magnesium citrate, or magnesium aspartate, in capsules or sublingual (under the tongue) drops. Encourage your partner to take the suggested dosage and increase the dosage daily. She should reduce her dosage if she feels fatigued, if her muscles feel weak, or if she experiences diarrhea. If your partner believes that she may be using too much magnesium, she can visit her physician for a blood test to evaluate the level of magnesium in her red blood cells. *If your partner has a history of kidney function problems, she should use magnesium only under the strict supervision of a physician.* Magnesium is safe for use when breastfeeding.

* Calcium depletes the body's supply of magnesium, which helps combat anxiety. If your partner is feeling anxious, suggest that she temporarily stop taking calcium supplements, including antacids and calcium-enriched foods such as orange juice.

* To help your partner reduce her anxiety, visit your local health food store for gamma-aminobutyric acid (GABA), a natural supplement that calms by stimulating the GABA receptor in the brain. Note, however, that some women do not respond to

this supplement and a very small number actually experience the opposite effect—they become a bit edgy for a few hours. GABA is safe for use when breastfeeding.

* Also visit your health food store for L-theanine, a supplement that relaxes and prevents agitation, and homeopathic remedies that help reduce anxiety naturally. Suggest that she use these products as directed anytime she feels anxious. L-theanine and homeopathic remedies are safe for use when breastfeeding.

* If your partner feels panicky at night, visit your local health food store or pharmacy for melatonin. Melatonin is a natural supplement that helps bring down high adrenaline levels. Your partner can take 1 milligram one-half hour before bedtime. This dosage may be increased daily by 1 milligram but should not exceed 7 milligrams. Most people will not tolerate more than 3 milligrams. Your partner should reduce the dosage if she finds that she rises too early, experiences disturbing dreams, or wakes up feeling groggy.

* Women with postpartum depression dominated by anxiety and panic respond extremely well to boosts of progesterone, often enjoying a mood turnaround in as few as twelve to twenty-four hours. Why? During pregnancy, a woman's body maintains an extremely high level of the progesterone hormone (100 times her usual level). Within hours after delivery, her progesterone level drops far below its pre-pregnancy level. This progesterone deficiency is often the reason women become depressed or anxious after delivery.

    Progesterone of this type may be purchased at a compounding pharmacy (a pharmacy that formulates specialized medications, including natural hormone preparations) and requires a prescription from her physician. Her initial dose of injectable progesterone should be 200 to 300 milligrams, depending on the severity of her mood, followed by progesterone capsules or sublingual (under the tongue) drops the following day. If she takes capsules, encourage her to take 100 milligrams every four to six hours as needed. If her dosage is too high, she is likely to feel dizzy or sleepy, warranting a change in dosage. Sublingual progesterone drops may be used in similar doses; progesterone cream does not yield the same results. Most women require another dose of injectable liquid progesterone every five to ten days for two to six weeks. Progesterone therapy should continue from six weeks to six months, as needed. Progesterone injections, capsules, and sublingual drops are safe for use when breastfeeding. See "Anxiety & Irritability Due to Progesterone Deficiency" (page 102) for more information.

* Like her progesterone level, your partner's estrogen levels also plummet immediately after delivery and have a tendency to affect her mood. However, in some cases, women suffering from postpartum depression dominated by anxiety and panic may not find supplementing estrogen helpful. In other cases, estrogen will significantly reduce episodes of anxiety and panic by decreasing the woman's production of epinephrine (a hormone produced by the adrenal gland). See "Postpartum Depression (Dominated by Depression)" (page 185) for information on how to supplement natural estrogen without side effects.

  If your partner takes natural estrogen supplements and feels that this therapy is exacerbating her condition by making her feel *more* anxious and panicky, encourage her to stop her treatment immediately. (The advantages of using natural hormones are that her body will immediately alert her if the substance is inappropriate, and the substance will leave her body in a few hours with no lingering effect—not in days or weeks as is the case with some pharmaceutical medications.)

* St. John's wort is another natural supplement that helps to elevate mood. Visit your local health food store for St. John's wort in .3 percent extract form. Suggest that your partner take 300 milliliters three times daily. *This remedy is not appropriate*

for new mothers who use an antidepressant medication in the SSRI category, such as Zoloft, Prozac, and Selexa. St. John's wort is safe for use when breastfeeding.

* The vitamin B family of supplements helps to improve mood and fight depression. Suggest that your partner take 1 milligram of vitamin B_{12} in sublingual (under the tongue) drops daily. She should also take 50 mg of a B complex vitamin.

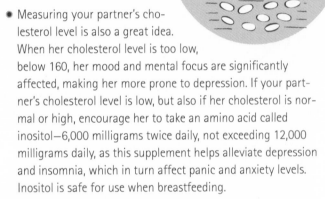

* Measuring your partner's cholesterol level is also a great idea. When her cholesterol level is too low, below 160, her mood and mental focus are significantly affected, making her more prone to depression. If your partner's cholesterol level is low, but also if her cholesterol is normal or high, encourage her to take an amino acid called inositol—6,000 milligrams twice daily, not exceeding 12,000 milligrams daily, as this supplement helps alleviate depression and insomnia, which in turn affect panic and anxiety levels. Inositol is safe for use when breastfeeding.

* Finally, visit your local health food store for other natural remedies that address anxiety, including Adaptogen products (including ginseng), Nux Vomica (a homeopathic remedy that promotes sleep and alleviates exhaustion; use as directed three to five times daily), and kava-kava (an herb that helps combat anxiety; choose a product derived from the *entire* kava-kava plant to protect your partner's liver; use as directed). These natural remedies may be used more often if anxiety or panic increases. They should not be used if your partner suffers from postpartum depression without anxiety and panic.

When to Get More Help:

For those women who would like to control their anxiety and panic attacks without the use of anti-anxiety medication, it is crucial that the natural aids recommended in this section be used *as soon as* anxiety begins; otherwise they may not be as effective. The idea is to break anxiety at its start—not hours later. New mothers should experiment *within the recommended dosages* to determine which amounts work best for their situation. If anxiety is not addressed immediately, it may be necessary for your partner to take a prescription medication such as Xanax or Ativan. These medications may be required for a few weeks of treatment but the need for them will likely fade as your partner becomes more comfortable with the various supplemental and behavioral methods available for controlling her anxiety.

If treatment has been delayed, encourage your partner to ask her physician about treating other conditions that may have developed incident to her anxiety, such as adrenal gland exhaustion. See "Fatigue Due to Adrenal Gland Exhaustion" (page 95) for more information.

If the recommendations outlined above are not helpful, contact your physician for additional assistance and a referral to a mental health professional. Don't hesitate to seek the support of family, friends, and organizations that assist families with postpartum depression.

Postpartum Depression (Dominated by Obsessive–Compulsive Feelings)

The Facts:

Postpartum depression comes in three different forms:

- postpartum depression dominated by feelings of depression

- postpartum depression dominated by feelings of anxiety and panic

- postpartum depression dominated by obsessive-compulsive feelings

Most women experience some combination of the conditions described above.

Postpartum depression dominated by obsessive-compulsive feelings is relatively uncommon. Women suffering from this type of postpartum depression often experience the following symptoms:

- obsessive worries about the health of the baby

- obsessive thoughts about their own health

- a preoccupation with cleanliness and germs

- a need to see the baby every few minutes in order to ensure that he is safe

- a reluctance to be alone with the baby due to fears of hurting him or her

This form of postpartum depression often goes unnoticed for some time, because new mothers tend to hide compulsive thoughts out of fear that their concerns will not be taken seriously or that they may actually be *crazy.*

! The symptoms of the three types of postpartum depression often overlap. Many women suffer from postpartum depression that includes symptoms of all three types. Once you and your partner identify what her symptoms are, simply incorporate the remedies suggested for those symptoms in the corresponding section.

What You Can Do:

LIFESTYLE CHANGES:

* First and foremost, recognize that your partner's mood changes are not voluntary. Postpartum depression is an unfortunate consequence of recovering from pregnancy and childbirth. She is experiencing an illness and requires your care and support. For more information, see "What Is It Like to Have Postpartum Depression?" (page 174).

* Open the line of communication between you. Postpartum depression is often characterized by feelings of loneliness, alienation, shame, and failure. Simply talking about these feelings is likely to help her feel better. Be kind; be patient; be encouraging. Tell her that you regard her as the most courageous woman you know. If you believe that you cannot be as available as you would like to be, arrange for her to speak to someone else—a friend, a family member, or a professional—who can regularly encourage her to speak about her feelings. Checking in with her regularly will also enable you to keep tabs on her mental state so that you can get additional help for her if her symptoms worsen.

* Make a plan to treat the whole woman—her mind (e.g., her emotional concerns), her body (e.g., her diet), and her lifestyle (e.g, the logistics associated with bringing home a new baby). All of these aspects of her life must be addressed simultaneously in order for her to feel that she is regaining control of her life.

* Assist your partner in getting more sleep. Sleep deprivation is a *major* contributor to feelings of depression—perhaps the most significant cause second to hormonal deficiencies. See "Sleep Deprivation & Insomnia" (page 76) and "A Parent's Guide to Adjusting to New Sleep Patterns" (page 228) for more information.

* Help your partner evaluate the many new responsibilities associated with having a baby. In earlier times, family members and friends would provide active assistance to new parents in the first few weeks, months, and years of a child's life, giving the mother support so that she could focus on recovering from childbirth and learning to care for her baby. Today, many couples live far from family and friends, and women wind up learning how to care for a baby on their own while healing from the delivery. Even if you are fortunate enough to have a support network on which to rely, help her determine how she will find time to sleep, exercise, eat properly, and spend time with friends. Provide as much assistance around the house as you can. See chapter 9, "Resuming Your Life Together," in this guidebook for more information.

* Eating simple, nutritious foods goes a long way toward helping the body and mind heal. When a body needn't expend extra energy processing the artificial colors, flavors, and chemicals in junk food, it can better perform the jobs of resting, repairing, and maintaining proper mental function. Encourage your partner to maintain a healthful diet and avoid processed foods. For more information on how you can help your partner eat well, see "Ideal Postpartum Diet" (page 148).

* Dehydration is a key culprit in depression. Encourage your partner to stay hydrated by drinking at least eight to twelve glasses of water daily, and even more if she is breastfeeding. Drinking water will help your partner's body cleanse itself of

the medications and other substances given during and after labor that can strongly affect mood and mental focus. Also encourage her to take hot baths and saunas. See "Maintaining Hydration" (page 123) for more information.

* Another effective means of cleansing her system is the consumption of diuretic foods. Encourage her to eat asparagus, cucumber, and parsley and drink tea made of dandelion infusion.

MEDICAL TESTING:

* Diet and proper nutrition have a great influence on a new mother's mood and sense of well-being. Besides watching what she eats, one way for the new mother to monitor whether she is eating well enough is to test her insulin level. Encourage her to visit her physician in order to check her fasting insulin level. If her insulin level is under 5, it is possible that your partner is not eating enough food in general or carbohydrates in particular.

* Suggest that she ask her physician to test her DHEAS level. This hormone plays an important role in maintaining women's hormonal balance, functioning as a strong antidepressant that also promotes stamina and strength. If your partner's DHEAS level is below 100, she is likely to benefit from supplementing this hormone. Ideally, she should begin by taking a 5-milligram pill per day and increase this dosage by 5 milligrams every two weeks, not exceeding 25 milligrams daily. Your partner should cut back her dosage if she begins to feel edgy or if her skin develops blemishes. DHEAS is safe for use when breastfeeding.

* Also encourage her to have her blood tested for the following:

  ⊙ electrolyte and CO_2 levels (check electrolyte balance and pH balance; see "Maintaining Hydration," page 123, for more information)

- ⊙ thyroid function (see "Preexisting Thyroid Disorder," page 88, and "Thyroid Disorder That Develops after Delivery," page 91, for more information)

- ⊙ iron (to ensure that she is not anemic)

SUPPLEMENTS

- ✳ Magnesium supplements are incredibly effective for alleviating depressive feelings and obsessive tendencies. Visit your local health food store for fast-absorbing magnesium, such as magnesium glycinate, magnesium gluconate, magnesium citrate, or magnesium aspartate, in capsules or sublingual (under the tongue) drops. Encourage your partner to take the suggested dosage and slowly increase the dosage every few days. She should reduce her dosage if she feels fatigued, if her muscles feel weak, or if she experiences diarrhea. If your partner believes that she may be using too much magnesium, she can visit her physician for a blood test to evaluate the level of magnesium in her red blood cells. *If your partner has a history of kidney function problems, she should use magnesium only under the strict supervision of a physician.* Magnesium is safe for use when breastfeeding.

- ✳ Calcium depletes the body's supply of magnesium, which helps combat obsessive tendencies. If your partner is experiencing this form of postpartum depression, suggest that she temporarily stop taking calcium supplements, including antacids and calcium-enriched foods such as orange juice.

- ✳ Women with postpartum depression dominated by obsessive and compulsive feelings respond extremely well to boosts of progesterone, often enjoying a mood turnaround in as few as twelve to twenty-four hours. Why? During pregnancy, a woman's body maintains an extremely high level of the progesterone hormone. Within hours after delivery, her progesterone level drops far below its pre-pregnancy level. This progesterone deficiency is often the reason women become depressed or obsessive after delivery. An emergency boost can address the very cause of her mood change—the drastic drop in progesterone—and make her feel better.

Progesterone of this type may be purchased at a compounding pharmacy (a pharmacy that formulates specialized medications, including natural hormone preparations) and requires a prescription from her physician. Her initial dose should be 200 to 300 milligrams of injectable progesterone, depending on the severity of her mood, followed by progesterone capsules or sublingual (under the tongue) drops the following day. If she takes capsules, encourage her to take 100 milligrams every four to six hours as needed. If her dosage is too high, she is likely to feel dizzy or sleepy, warranting a change in dosage. Sublingual progesterone drops may be used in similar doses; progesterone cream does not yield the same results. Most women require another dose of liquid progesterone every five to ten days for two to six weeks. Progesterone therapy should continue from six weeks to six months, as needed. Progesterone injections, capsules, and sublingual drops are safe for use when breastfeeding. See "Anxiety & Irritability Due to Progesterone Deficiency" (page 102) for more information.

* Like her progesterone level, your partner's estrogen levels also plummet immediately after delivery and have a tendency to affect her mood. However, in some cases, women suffering from postpartum depression dominated by obsessive and compulsive feelings may not find supplementing estrogen helpful. In other cases, estrogen will significantly reduce episodes of depression and compulsion by decreasing the woman's production of epinephrine (a hormone produced by the adrenal gland). See "Postpartum Depression (Dominated by Depression)" (page 185) for information on how to supplement natural estrogen without side effects.

If your partner takes natural estrogen supplements and feels that this therapy is exacerbating her condition by making her feel *more* anxious, with no reduction in her compulsive episodes, encourage her to stop her treatment immediately. (The advantages of using natural hormones are that her body will immediately alert her if the substance is inappropriate, and the substance will leave her body in a few hours with no lingering effect—not in days or weeks as is the case with some pharmaceutical medications.)

* Above all, remember that postpartum depression rarely falls into one category. Mix and match your remedies as based on the various symptoms your partner experiences. For more information, see chapter 7, "An Overview of Postpartum Depression" in this guidebook.

When to Get More Help:

Any time symptoms of postpartum depression or compulsive and obsessive behavior appear to be growing worse over time, contact your partner's physician for additional help and a referral to a mental health professional.

If treatment has been delayed, encourage your partner to ask her physician about treating other conditions that may have developed incident to her anxiety, such as adrenal gland exhaustion. See "Fatigue Due to Adrenal Gland Exhaustion" (page 95) for more information.

Don't hesitate to seek the support of family, friends, and organizations that assist families with postpartum depression.

Postpartum Psychosis

The Facts:

Postpartum psychosis is the most extreme form of postpartum mood change, but fortunately it is experienced by less than 1 percent of new mothers. This condition may begin as early as the third or fourth day after delivery and include symptoms of postpartum depression, but it *also* includes the following symptoms:

- ⊙ hallucinations (hearing voices or seeing things that aren't there)

- ⊙ manic episodes

- ⊙ a disconnection between actual events and her perception of those events

- ⊙ a worsening of these symptoms

While rare, postpartum psychosis is *extremely* dangerous. A woman suffering from this condition presents an *immediate* danger to herself, to her partner, her other children, and her newborn. In general, these women are treated in the hospital for several weeks or months.

What You Can Do:

* Always take seriously any signs that your partner is responding irrationally to her new role as a mother. These may be the first signs of this dangerous condition. If she displays any of the symptoms of psychosis, *immediately* contact her physician for a referral to a mental health professional.

* Many women who suffer from postpartum psychosis must spend several weeks or months in the hospital. Once they get their initial psychosis under control, it is common for them to return home and experience postpartum *depression,* for the

very same reasons that led to the psychosis. See "Postpartum Depression (Dominated by Depression)" (page 185) for information on how you can assist her with the transition back to home life.

* Your partner may find that if she receives estrogen and progesterone therapy she recovers from her psychosis more quickly *and* avoids developing postpartum depression upon her release from the hospital. Encourage her to ask her physician or psychiatrist about hormone replacement therapy (or ask on her behalf) while she is being treated for postpartum psychosis. Recent studies confirm the benefits of estrogen treatment for postpartum psychosis.

* If your partner is hospitalized, you will likely feel overwhelmed by the stress of dealing with your partner's illness and your new responsibilities as a father. This is not the time for you to try to be a "single parent" and do everything yourself. Instead, accept offers of help from family and friends.

* Finally, recognize that your partner is suffering from a debilitating but probably temporary illness. Be understanding and patient. With the proper, immediate treatment, the woman you love *will* return to care for you, your new baby, and your family. For now, do what you can to care for her.

When to Get More Help:

It is not possible to treat postpartum psychosis at home. If your partner displays any of the symptoms of psychosis described above, *they will not go away and she will only grow to be more dangerous to you, herself, your newborn, and your other children.* Immediately contact her physician for a referral to a mental health professional.

Postpartum Post-Traumatic Stress Disorder

The Facts:

For some women, the events that transpire during labor and delivery are so traumatic that they emerge from the experience with symptoms of post-traumatic stress disorder (PTSD), including

- ⊙ flashbacks that cause them to temporarily lose their sense of reality as they relive the event

- ⊙ nightmares

- ⊙ feelings of helplessness

- ⊙ feelings of fear

- ⊙ panic attacks

The kinds of events that might cause a new mother to exhibit these symptoms include an especially painful delivery; a sudden, unexpected C-section; and severe bleeding after delivery that requires a great deal of medical assistance from her medical staff. Any of these can be jarring during an already sensitive time.

? Why do these seemingly "normal" labor-related events become traumatic events for some women? While most mothers are prepared for pregnancy, few women know what labor is *really* like and what to expect in the heat of the action. Most women assume that childbirth will be like the births they have seen in movies. Unfortunately, real-life deliveries, even at their easiest, are far more painful and difficult than those that are depicted in movies. If their actual delivery turns out to be significantly more complicated or difficult than they expected, the shock, fear, and vulnerability associated with the event can cause considerable stress for some women.

What You Can Do:

* If your partner experienced a significantly traumatic delivery, be prepared for mood changes that may be more properly attributed to post-traumatic stress disorder than to postpartum depression. Look out for the symptoms listed above so that you can arrange for treatment when she needs it.

* Speak to her about what occurred during her delivery. Try to understand her perspective. Share your perspective with her. In many cases, talking about the labor and expressing her feelings can go a long way toward making her feel better about the event.

* Be her advocate. If you see that your partner is not able to act on her own behalf, alert her physician to your suspicions in order to allow him or her to adjust treatment accordingly.

When to Get More Help:

If you believe that your partner's mood changes are related to the events of her labor, make a point of speaking to her physician so that her care may be better directed.

Preventing Postpartum Depression & Psychosis after Future Pregnancies

The Facts:

A new mother who has experienced postpartum depression after one pregnancy is likely to experience it again after future pregnancies. In fact, the rate of recurrence of postpartum psychosis is as high as 25 percent.

Of course, having experienced your partner's postpartum mood changes following a previous pregnancy, you will be more likely to know what to expect—*and* how to quickly provide treatment when the symptoms reappear. The advantage of this is that early detection and prompt treatment often prevent these symptoms from becoming more pronounced and help them subside far more quickly.

Nearly thirty years ago, Dr. Katrina Dalton proposed a connection between the drop in progesterone after delivery and postpartum mood changes. She suggested that taking progesterone supplements in subsequent pregnancies could prevent the recurrence of this condition. Physicians who follow her protocol have found that postpartum depression does not occur as frequently in women who have been given progesterone before giving birth.

What You Can Do:

LIFESTYLE CHANGES:

* Assist your partner in getting more sleep. Sleep deprivation is a *major* contributor to feelings of depression—perhaps the most significant cause second to hormonal deficiencies. See "Sleep Deprivation & Insomnia" (page 76) and "A Parent's Guide to Adjusting to New Sleep Patterns" (page 228) for more information.

* Help your partner evaluate the many new responsibilities associated with having a baby. In earlier times, family members and friends would provide active assistance to new parents in the first few weeks, months, and years of a child's life, giving the mother support so that she could focus on recovering from childbirth and learning to care for and get to know her new baby. Even more help was typically offered after a second pregnancy, as grandmothers and aunts volunteered to watch the first child, prepare meals, and take care of household chores while the mother rested and recovered from the birth, attended to her new baby, or bathed. Today, many couples live far from family and friends, and women wind up having to care for their new baby *and* their older children on their own— all while trying to recover from the delivery. Even if you are fortunate enough to have a support network on which to rely, help her determine how she will find time to recover, sleep, exercise, eat properly, spend time with friends, and care for her older children without being pulled in too many directions. Provide as much assistance around the house as you can. See chapter 9, "Resuming Your Life Together," in this guidebook for more information.

* Open the line of communication between you. Allow her to express her feelings about the possible return of her postpartum depression. Be supportive and reassure her that what you and she handled once can be handled again—this time only faster.

* Make a plan to treat the whole woman—her mind (e.g., her emotional concerns), her body (e.g., her diet), and her lifestyle (e.g, the logistics associated with bringing home a new baby). All of these aspects of her life must be addressed simultaneously in order for her to feel that she is regaining control of her life.

* Diet and proper nutrition have a great influence on a new mother's mood and sense of well-being. Besides watching what she eats, one way for the new mother to monitor whether she is eating well enough is to test her insulin level. Encourage her to visit her physician in order to check her fasting insulin level. If her insulin level is under 5, it is possible that your partner is not eating enough food in general or carbohydrates in particular.

MEDICAL TESTING:

* Suggest that she ask her physician to test her DHEAS level. This hormone plays an important role in maintaining women's hormonal balance, functioning as a strong antidepressant that also promotes stamina and strength. If your partner's DHEAS level is below 100, she is likely to benefit from supplementing this hormone. Ideally, she should begin by taking a 5-milligram pill per day and increase this dosage by 5 milligrams every two weeks, not exceeding 25 milligrams daily. Your partner should cut back her dosage if she begins to feel edgy or if her skin develops blemishes. DHEAS is safe for use when breastfeeding.

* Also encourage her to have her blood tested for the following:

  ⊙ electrolyte and CO_2 levels (check electrolyte balance and pH balance; see "Maintaining Hydration," page 123, for more information)

  ⊙ thyroid function (see "Preexisting Thyroid Disorder," page 88, and "Thyroid Disorder That Develops after Delivery," page 91, for more information)

  ⊙ iron (to ensure that she is not anemic)

SUPPLEMENTS:

* During pregnancy, women's bodies maintain an extremely high level of the progesterone and estrogen hormones. Within hours after the delivery, both estrogen and progesterone drop

far below pre-pregnancy levels. More than 20 years ago, English physician Katherine Dalton demonstrated that injecting progesterone, beginning in the 34th week of pregnancy, can prevent postpartum depression and postpartum psychosis. Recent studies have shown that providing patients with estrogen supplements immediately after the delivery can also decrease the incidents of postpartum depression and postpartum psychosis.

Consider speaking to your partner and her physician about combining these two tried-and-true treatments to prevent the recurrence of postpartum depression and postpartum psychosis in a new pregnancy.

Your partner may begin receiving 200 milligram injections of liquid progesterone (in oil) in her 34th and 36th weeks of pregnancy, followed by weekly 200 milligram injections until her delivery and daily injections for the first four to five days after the baby is born. If your partner's mood seems well at the end of her first week after the delivery, she may scale down her injections from daily to weekly, and continue these injections for six weeks.

Estrogen is supplemented in a gel form called Triest (a combination of E1 [0.25 milligrams]), E2 [0.75 milligrams] and E3 [2.5 milligrams], which equal one gram of gel). Your partner should rub 0.75 to two grams of gel over her inner arms, palms, face, and neck twice per day, immediately after her delivery.

Your partner should continue using the Triest gel for two to three weeks following delivery and begin reducing the amount she uses in the third or fourth week following delivery. If your partner decreases her dosage of either progesterone or estrogen and experiences a return of postpartum depression and postpartum psychosis symptoms, encourage her to increase her dosage of these natural hormonal supplements and refer to the supplements recommended in the "Postpartum Depression (Dominated by Depression)," page 185.

* Prepare, prepare, prepare. Many couples face the same problems repeatedly because they don't want to admit that unpleasant times can return. Of course, with a second, third, or fourth child, family members and friends become less enthusiastic about extending support, which only makes things more difficult for the couple. If you know what may lie ahead, make a plan for how you will deal with the various postpartum mood changes and baby-related logistics that you can expect.

* Finally, a woman who has suffered significant postpartum depression should *never* be pressured to get pregnant again, regardless of previous plans you have made to have a certain number of children. If the subject of a subsequent pregnancy does arise, make sure that it is *her* idea. Then treat her pregnancy as a mutual project that includes planning for the possible return of postpartum depression.

When to Get More Help:

If your partner suffered from postpartum depression following a previous pregnancy but finds that her physician is not informed about or open to preventing it with natural progesterone and estrogen therapy—preferring instead to reassure her that all will be well this time—suggest that she either encourage her current physician to learn about this type of therapy or consult another obstetrician.

The New Mother's Life

The Challenges of Balancing Baby, Self & Partner

9 RESUMING YOUR LIFE TOGETHER

Getting Your Baby to Sleep

The Facts:

Getting a baby to fall asleep easily and stay asleep long enough to allow the parents to get some sleep is one parenting success that dramatically improves the quality of life for new mothers and fathers.

? How much do newborns sleep? You can expect your baby to sleep approximately seventeen to eighteen hours a day at one week of age, and approximately sixteen to seventeen hours a day at one month of age. Unfortunately, this sleep is generally broken up into several two- to four-hour blocks throughout the day and night. As your baby gets older, her sleep will gradually consolidate into longer blocks of time, with the longest block of time taking place during the night. Most babies are physically able to sleep through the night (i.e., six hours at a time) by three to six months.

Of course, many babies sleep significantly less, and less consistently, than their parents expect them to. Over the first weeks and months following the baby's arrival, consistent sleep disruption and deprivation begin to take their toll on the new mother and father, often resulting in:

- ⊙ parental exhaustion

- ⊙ tension in the parents' relationship

- ⊙ a delay in the resumption of intimate contact

- ⊙ a reduction in the frequency of intimate contact

- ⊙ a tendency for mothers to terminate breastfeeding earlier than planned

- ⊙ a tendency for mothers to forgo breastfeeding in subsequent pregnancies

- the decision not to
  have another child

- the development of
  anxiety and depression, including "baby
  blues," postpartum
  depression, or postpartum psychosis

Moreover, the problems
caused by a baby's less-than-ideal sleep patterns tend to grow rather than diminish with time. More often than not, problematic bedtime routines established during the early months tend to evolve into higher-maintenance sleep habits as the child grows older—habits that often adversely affect a couple's relationship.

? How can a young baby's sleep routines become destructive to his parents' relationship? Consider the following example. A baby boy grows accustomed to being rocked to sleep by his mother and then being transferred to his crib. As the years progress and he grows bigger and heavier, transferring him to his bed becomes more difficult, so his mother puts him into his bed awake and stays with him until he falls asleep. Often she falls asleep with him and returns to spend the rest of the night with her partner several hours later. The child's need for his mother's presence in order to fall asleep prevents the parents from having time alone together in the evening. Making love is out of the question. Since it is common for the boy to join his parents in their bed when he first awakens in the morning, intimacy early in the morning when his parents first wake up is also impossible. Their only option for romance is for the mother to wake her partner when she returns to their bed in the middle of the night, but this is not an ideal situation. The child's sleep habits clearly have had a destructive effect on his parents' relationship.

Is there a magic formula that can help your child fall asleep with little trouble and stay asleep until morning? If there were, you would have already heard about it. Instead, when you research the subject you will probably find a variety of philosophies and tools espoused by pediatricians, baby sleep authorities, and experienced mothers and fathers. The key is for you to find the formula that works for your baby and your family.

What You Can Do:

PREPARATION:

* Before your baby arrives, take time to learn about babies' typical sleep needs and patterns, so you can know what to expect from your newborn. Consult friends, on-line resource centers, baby-care books, and infant-sleep books. Below are some helpful resources:

  ⊙ *On Becoming Baby Wise: Learn How over 500,000 Babies Were Trained to Sleep through the Night the Natural Way* by Gary Ezzo and Robert Buckman, M.D.

  ⊙ *Secrets of the Baby Whisperer: How to Calm, Connect and Communicate with Your Baby* by Tracy Hogg with Melinda Blau

  ⊙ *The Happiest Baby on the Block: The New Way to Calm Crying and Help Your Baby Sleep Longer* by Harvey Karp, M.D.

  ⊙ *Mothering the New Mother: Women's Feelings & Needs after Childbirth: A Support & Resource Guide* by Sally Placksin

  ⊙ *The Girlfriends' Guide to Surviving the First Year of Motherhood* by Vicky Iovine

  In each of these and other helpful resources, you're likely to find one of three main philosophies governing how parents may respond to the cries and sleep needs of their baby:

- ⊙ Do everything necessary to ensure that the baby doesn't cry.

- ⊙ Let the baby "cry it out."

- ⊙ Consider the baby's cry a communication tool letting you know when he needs to be fed, changed, held, or put to bed.

Each of these three philosophies differs greatly from the others. Discuss these philosophies with your partner and together adopt a philosophy that suits you. This will guide you as you develop your *initial* game plan.

* Consider volunteering to babysit for friends who have a young baby. In the process you will learn firsthand about babies' needs and sleeping patterns *and* gain the added benefit of having this couple return the favor after your baby arrives.

* Ask the parents you know to tell you how they initially planned to get their baby to sleep, what problems they encountered, and how they ultimately resolved these challenges. Take a class on baby sleep at your local parenting resource center, if one is offered. Consult books, articles, and on-line resource centers to find out how other parents have dealt with the problem of their infants' sleep. For every solution you hear or read about, ask yourself whether it fits the philosophy you have adopted. Also consider what kind of relationship you want with your child—do you favor attachment parenting (which involves "wearing" the baby most of the day and sharing your bed with him or her at night) or more traditional parenting practices? Do you want to have your baby fall asleep in your bed every night? Will your partner want to nurse the baby to sleep before every nap? Will you both prefer to have the baby fall asleep on his or her own? Undoubtedly you will want your child to sleep well but also be social, functional, and generally well adjusted.

* Once you decide on your initial game plan, also make a backup plan in case your original plan doesn't work. Then make a second backup plan. When you find yourself up at three o'clock in the morning for the fiftieth night in a row, you're likely to do *anything* that will get your baby to fall asleep. By simply taking the time to plan for the "failure" of your original strategy, the solution you choose in the middle of the night will more likely be consistent with what works for your family—and it will probably be more successful, to boot.

* Encourage your partner to supplement her diet with capsules of fish oil, specifically docosahexaenoic acid (DHA) and eicosapentaenoic acid (EPA), in late pregnancy. Studies indicate that both of these natural substances enhance baby brain development *and* stabilize baby sleep patterns! You can obtain capsules containing a combination of docosahexaenoic acid (DHA) and eicosapentaenoic acid (EPA) at your local health food store or pharmacy. Look for a supplement that clearly indicates that the product has low mercury levels. Encourage your partner to take 1,000 to 2,000 milligrams twice daily.

! Sudden Infant Death Syndrome (SIDS) is a serious risk facing all newborns. Even the most attentive parents can inadvertently endanger their baby if they are not familiar with the various SIDS-related dangers. Do your homework in order to ensure that you:
    • put your baby to sleep on her back
    • do not overdress your baby before bedtime and naptime
    • keep the crib free of blankets, pillows, and toys and avoid other potentially deadly SIDS hazards

ACTION:

* When your newborn baby resists falling asleep or cries in the middle of the night, refer to and follow your plan of action. Be confident. Even if you don't *feel* prepared, remind yourself that both of you are equipped to give your baby everything he or she needs.

* On the other hand, recognize that your baby is neither a sack of potatoes nor a computer. He will respond to your actions, unlike a sack of potatoes, but perhaps not instantly, as a computer would. Be patient. You will eventually get enough sleep. Don't focus your frustration on the baby—his crying is neither your fault nor his.

* Just as adults do, babies require darkness in order for their bodies to produce melatonin and sleep deeply. When you put your baby to sleep, draw the curtains to make the room as dark as possible.

* If your baby is fussy and has trouble sleeping, it is possible that he is not getting enough breast milk. If your partner thinks this may be possible, encourage her to see a lactation consultant to make sure the baby is latching on and nursing properly and feeding often enough. See chapter 5, "Breastfeeding," in this guidebook for more information.

* As you learn more about your baby's sleeping, eating, and crying patterns, keep your partner—and any other caregiver—informed. Everyone who is on your baby's "team" should have the most up-to-date intelligence on how to best understand and meet your baby's needs.

When to Get More Help:

The minute you feel that you have exhausted your resources, ask for help. Baby nurses, baby sleep experts, pediatricians, and experienced relatives and friends may have the answers you need. *Keep* looking for solutions until your baby's sleep patterns allow you to get enough sleep so that you can function properly.

If your baby does not gradually extend the number of hours she sleeps, consult your pediatrician.

A Parent's Guide to Adjusting to New Sleep Patterns

The Facts:

Just as your baby requires sleep, so do you and your partner. Sleep is essential for normal functioning. Lack of sleep will quickly erode your enjoyment of this magical time with your newborn, in addition to increasing your partner's chances of suffering from postpartum mood changes, making you both less effective during the day (and night), and putting a strain on your relationship.

The recommendations provided in this section are based on the assumption that the new mother will either stay at home or take a six-week maternity leave, and that you, her partner, will take a one-week paternity leave.

What You Can Do:

DURING YOUR PATERNITY LEAVE:

* Most of the time, there is no reason for both parents to wake up during the night to comfort or feed the baby. For the sake of your stamina for the long journey of parenthood ahead of you, agree that only one parent will be awake at a time. (Be flexible, though—there will be times when your partner has been trying to calm your screaming baby for hours and really needs a break. If she wakes you and asks for help, give her the help she needs.)

* If the sleeping parent is kept awake by the baby's cries, pick up a pair of earplugs at your local pharmacy and use them.

? How can you—the non-breastfeeding parent—care for the baby's needs in the middle of the night? As soon as possible, when your partner is producing enough milk and the baby has settled into a comfortable nursing technique (usually three to four weeks), your partner can begin using a breast pump to express milk during the day so you can give the baby a bottle during the night. However, note that even as soon as the first few days back home, if you see that your new mother is exhausted and displays the early symptoms of depression, encourage her to use a breast pump immediately. After all, waiting three or four weeks before suggesting a remedy for her sleeplessness may cause her to give up breastfeeding altogether in favor of a better night's sleep—and more dangerous still, since lack of sleep is a key culprit in the onset of postpartum depression, waiting those few weeks may cause her emotional state to deteriorate unnecessarily. See "Breast-feeding & Pumping When She Returns to Work" (page 141) for more information.

* It is common for new mothers to want to "do it all." Your partner may claim that she can manage nighttime parenting all on her own. If this is the case with your partner, keep an eye on or ask her about her energy level. If you know she hasn't slept for several nights or she begins to look haggard, insist on taking over for a night or two to allow her to catch up on her sleep. Remind her that there is nothing heroic about being so exhausted that she cannot function—your baby needs her to be in top form.

* Maximizing your and your partner's opportunities to sleep may mean waking up your baby from time to time. For example, if your baby falls asleep before he has fed enough, don't be afraid to wake him up to ensure that he gets a full feeding—otherwise he will probably wake you again in an hour or so. Similarly, if he fed at ten o'clock and is not due for another feeding until one o'clock in the morning but you would like to go to sleep at midnight, don't be afraid to wake him for another feeding—this might just allow you to sleep until three o'clock!

AFTER YOU RETURN TO WORK:

* Once you return to work outside of the home, it may be more difficult for you to stay up at night with your baby and still function well the following morning. On the other hand, absent a live-in caregiver's help at night, it is still important for you to help your partner get the sleep that she needs. Try the following schedule:

  ⊙ Although you may be tired from working all week, take over for your partner on Friday and Saturday nights.

  ⊙ Catch up on sleep during the day on weekends.

  ⊙ Your partner goes back on night duty Sunday and Monday nights.

  ⊙ On Tuesday, Wednesday, and Thursday nights, try to return home at a reasonable hour in order to give your partner a chance to nap until midnight or two in the morning, at which time she goes back on duty and you go to sleep.

  By adhering to the schedule above, both you and your partner will be able to care for the baby, meet your other obligations, and avoid complete exhaustion.

* The idea that a mother and father must care for their newborn alone is a relatively recent development of modern American life. Traditionally, an entire extended family would pitch in to help a couple get enough sleep during the first months of their baby's life. If you are lucky enough to have friends and family members who offer to help you during the first few months, don't be proud—accept happily. Your relationship with your baby, other children, and partner will benefit!

* If you have the good fortune to have a family member or baby nurse assist you for the first few weeks of your baby's life, avoid a crisis by planning your work and sleep schedule *before* this person leaves.

* As you learn more about your baby's sleeping, eating, and crying patterns, keep your partner—and any other caregiver—informed. Everyone who is on your baby's "team" should have the most up-to-date intelligence on how to best understand and meet your baby's needs.

When to Get More Help:

If you are not able to take a paternity leave, if you cannot reduce your sleep and still maintain your focus at work, or if your partner is suffering from postpartum depression, don't give up. Make it possible for you both to get enough sleep by asking family members or friends to take turns helping out at night or by offering to watch friends' or relatives' children in exchange for their help at night. If you don't have an extended family or circle of friends, ask your clergyperson if he or she knows of capable and trustworthy church members who might be willing to help.

Creating a Family Bed

The Facts:

The idea of a "co-sleeping," or sleeping in a "family bed," is not new. In Japan, for example, it is common for families to share a bed far into their children's adolescence. One of the reasons this concept has gained popularity among women in North America is simple—new mothers are exhausted. Keeping the baby in the bed, where the baby can be easily fed during night without the mother having to get up, is very inviting. Despite the convenience and many advantages associated with this sleeping practice, co-sleeping in a family bed has become quite controversial.

Medical risks are associated with sleeping in a family bed. Accidental child crushing and suffocation by exhausted mothers and fathers occur with enough frequency (most commonly between the second and fourth months of the baby's life) to worry medical professionals. Although proponents of the family bed concept claim that co-sleeping reduces the incidence of Sudden Infant Death Syndrome (SIDS), this claim is not supported by studies conducted by the American Academy of Pediatrics and the National Institute of Child Health and Human Development—which indicate that sleeping in a family bed may actually *increase* the incidents of SIDS.

Sleep quality may also be affected by co-sleeping. Sleep experts and childhood development scholars indicate that the family bed may actually *decrease* sleep for both babies and parents, due to the baby's tendency to stay awake in expectation of the parents' attention and the parents' difficulty relaxing due to their awareness of the baby's presence. Alternatively, some babies fall asleep easier in the family bed but do not sleep as deeply because they are roused slightly by their parents' ordinary sleep movements and noises.

Some child development experts propose that having a baby sleep in a separate bed or a separate room builds confidence in the child. Other family therapy professionals frown upon the family bed as a "contraceptive crutch" used by parents in order to avoid confronting the issue of sexual intimacy.

Due to the contentious nature of this subject, you are likely to hear passionate arguments for and against the family bed, depending on whom you speak to. Educate yourselves about the pros and cons of the family bed and act in a manner that best suits your family.

? What about using bassinets that attach to the parents bed, preventing you or your partner from rolling over onto the baby or blocking her breathing? These add-on beds, also called Co-Sleepers, may allow families to enjoy the closeness and convenience of keeping the baby in the bed without the medical risks. If you and your partner choose to use one of these add-on beds, make sure that you install it correctly and that your baby stays in the protected area.

What You Can Do:

* Consult the early-childhood resources recommended in "Getting Your Baby to Sleep" (page 222). Solicit the advice of family and friends who have shared their bed with their children. What has worked for them? Do you consider their children to be well adjusted, happy, and confident?

* If you and your partner have chosen to establish a family bed, make sure that the arrangement actually *works* for you. Remember that one of the major reasons for creating a family bed is to allow the new mother and father to sleep for longer periods of time. If having your baby in bed with you does not result in more sleep for you—or worse, if your baby's presence in the bed actually wakes your partner up more often—perhaps you and your partner should reevaluate whether co-sleeping is right for your family.

* Be very mindful of how the co-sleeping arrangement affects your ability to be intimate with your partner. If having your baby in the bed means that your partner is not interested in sex, speak to her about this issue. A family bed should never get in the way of a couple's physical intimacy.

* If you and your partner never intended to co-sleep, but the nighttime needs of your baby lead you to practice co-sleeping out of convenience, take an opportunity to discuss this development. How does your partner feel about having a third person in your bed? How do you feel about it? Don't put off having this conversation because you hesitate to express concerns that may seem "unfatherly."

When to Get More Help:

If you find that you and your partner have conflicting ideas about the family bed, if you have trouble communicating your feelings about having your newborn in your bed, or if you find that maintaining a family bed is affecting your intimate relationship, consult with a family therapist as quickly as possible. Don't allow weeks to slip by. Get help in order to resume communicating with and relating to your partner as lovers.

Managing Housework

The Facts:

Even while you rejoice in the arrival of your newborn, housework still needs to be done. You can make a significant contribution to the smooth functioning of your household during the first few weeks while your partner recovers from childbirth, and beyond. While every family will address this issue in a manner that works for them, a few guidelines can apply to every household.

What You Can Do:

* Ideally, a large extended family will help you and your partner care for your newborn and manage the housework. Or your mother or mother-in-law might stay with you to help out for a few weeks. If this is not an option for your family, ask a friend or family member to come in regularly and help with laundry, shopping, and other chores. Make sure you and your partner show your gratitude by offering a thoughtful thank-you gift or doing a similar favor for them.

* Even if you did not assist with the housework before your baby was born, *do* help out now. Ask your partner each day if there are particular jobs she would like done. Simply taking the time to ask your partner about her preferences will help her relax and recover *in addition* to reminding her how lucky she is to have you as a partner.

* Assess your family's housecleaning expectations. What level of "clean" do you and your partner require in order to feel comfortable? A messy, disorganized house may prevent your partner from getting the rest she needs—she may feel obligated to spend her recovery time cleaning. If you are unable to keep the house clean enough, make arrangements for housecleaning chores to be done by family members, friends, or a professional.

* If you and your partner can tolerate some disorganization around your home for a period of time, consider using the following shortcuts and commonsense tips:

  ⊙ Order food in, or purchase healthy prepared food from the supermarket. Alternatively, friends or family members may want to stock your freezer with homemade meals.

  ⊙ If your budget allows, send your laundry out. Many laundry services also pick up and deliver. Alternatively, ask a friend, family member, or neighbor to assist with the laundry in exchange for a similar service in the future. Try to make this arrangement before your baby arrives.

  ⊙ When you use a household object, make a point of returning it to its place immediately.

  ⊙ Each day, spend fifteen minutes clearing off surfaces in a different room. You'll be surprised at how much of an impact just fifteen minutes can make!

  ⊙ Make arrangements for someone to help you pay your bills during the first month of your newborn's life. If possible, make double payments in the month prior to his arrival.

* Be flexible. If your partner used to prepare a full breakfast for you each day, realize that you may have to forgo this special treatment while your partner recovers and adjusts to life with a newborn. And even if you must eat takeout dinners on paper plates, keep in mind that you are still sitting together and enjoying each other's company.

When to Get More Help:

Whenever you or your partner feels overwhelmed by the amount of housework required, ask for assistance from a family member, friend, neighbor, or professional.

Addressing the Needs of Your Other Children

The Facts:

Most mothers will tell you that caring for a second baby is easier than caring for the first. After all, by the time the second child comes along, a mother is more confident, knows what to expect, and is more attuned to the subtle signals of a newborn.

Of course, having a second child also means that your partner cannot fully focus on her new baby—she must also attend to the needs of her first child. Additionally, the first child is likely to have strong feelings and reactions around the arrival of a sibling, requiring parents to address these feelings and help the child adjust to this significant change in his or her life and family structure.

What You Can Do:

PREPARATION:

* Prior to the arrival of your second baby, inform your older child about the new sibling. Talk about what it will be like to have a new baby in the house and how he or she may feel as a result. Listen to your child's concerns and fears, and continually let him or her know that your love is unconditional.

* Arrange for your child to spend time with another child around her age who has a younger sibling.

* If the hospital where your partner will give birth offers a class for older siblings, arrange for your child to attend this class. Some hospitals even allow an older child to spend the night in the room with his mother after the baby is born.

* Take the time to make child-care arrangements with family members or friends, both during the time when your partner

will be in the hospital and in the weeks after she gives birth. Make a post-delivery child-care schedule for your older child, including grandparents, aunts, cousins, and neighbors if possible. To make the transition easier for your child, begin this schedule prior to the arrival of the baby. See "Managing Child Care with the Help of Your Extended 'Family'" (page 240) for more information.

* In addition to arranging for child care, don't forget to help your partner delegate responsibilities related to your older child, such as driving a carpool and contributing snacks at his or her preschool.

* Finally, recognize that the arrival of a newborn is probably even more overwhelming to your older child than it is for you. This is a time to limit changes (and reduce expectations) in an older sibling's life as much as possible, since he or she will need all available resources in order to deal with the dramatic transition and life changes that lay ahead. Keep your family's routines as stable and predictable as possible, so your older child can know what to expect and count on.

ACTION:

* When your baby arrives, be mindful that your older child receives plenty of attention from you, your partner, and visitors. When friends come to see the new baby, suggest that they first greet your older child. It can be helpful to have a basket stocked with inexpensive wrapped gifts, so that the older child has a present to open whenever visitors arrive bearing gifts for the new baby.

* If your child is old enough, consider including her in the process of welcoming home and caring for the new baby. For example, ask her to bring you a diaper or baby wipe during changing time. As your older child grows, she can contribute more according to her ability and interest.

* If you and your partner are not able to arrange for sufficient child care, and if your local school system allows, consider enrolling your older child in school a bit earlier than you otherwise would.

* Recognize that the behavior of your older child may change in reaction to the arrival of a sibling. In the first few weeks or months, it is not uncommon for older children to:

  ⊙ experience toilet-learning regression

  ⊙ return to throwing tantrums, sucking their thumbs, and other behaviors typical of a baby or younger child

  ⊙ begin a defiant phase

This behavior is usually temporary and will fade as your older child adjusts to his or her new role as an older brother or sister. Receiving lots of affection, praise, reassurance, and consistent discipline from you and your partner will help speed your child's adjustment process.

When to Get More Help:

If you find that your older child requires more attention than you, your partner, and your child-care assistants are able to give—or that his or her behavior is extremely aggressive, dangerous, or worrisome in any way—turn to friends, family, books, on-line resources, and your pediatrician for assistance.

Managing Child Care with the Help of Your Extended "Family"

The Facts:

In the past, a new mother and father were not required to care for a newborn on their own. A whole network of relatives, friends, and neighbors assisted in caring for the baby, caring for older children, preparing meals, doing household chores, and generally assisting in the new mother's education and recovery.

Today, this high level of support from an extended family may not be available to all new parents. However, it may be possible for you to create this kind of support system in time for the arrival of your newborn. In order to do this, consider that an "extended family" can easily include friends, neighbors, "adopted" parents and grandparents, and coworkers.

Creating a network of helpers is particularly useful for single parents and families in which one parent is required to be away from home for long periods. Even if you and your partner have family members living close by, your family will still benefit from expanding your support network as much as possible.

What You Can Do:

* If you and your partner live far from your immediate relatives, consider asking whether they know of any extended family members who live near you. You may discover that you or your partner has a relative living close by who would love to get to know you and help out.

* The arrival of a child is often an ideal time to review or work out conflicts with parents and adult siblings, in order to reduce stress and benefit from extended family support.

* Often, lonely—but competent and trustworthy—older neighbors or fellow church members would love to become an

"adopted" grandparent. Before the arrival of your child, ask your neighbors and your clergyperson if they know of any such older people who might be willing to help.

* Offer to serve as extended family members to friends and neighbors. Offer to watch or transport their kids in exchange for a similar kindness in the future.

* Parent groups and on-line communities can also serve as a form of extended family, providing information and support to new parents.

When to Get More Help:

Of course, in some cases help from extended family can become overwhelming, especially in those cases where a grandparent oversteps the bounds of what is comfortable for a new mother. This is particularly troublesome when a new mother is being cared for by a well-meaning mother-in-law and does not feel comfortable expressing displeasure at some aspect of this woman's generous help. Be your partner's advocate. Speak to her about how you can help create balance between the family member who would like to help and the new mother who requires help, privacy, respect, and some measure of autonomy.

Pets & Your New Baby

The Facts:

When you bring your new baby home, you, your partner, and your older children are not the only ones who must undergo a transition—your pets also experience a period of adjustment during this time. Previously docile pets, unaccustomed to sharing your affection, may suddenly act in a territorial manner or become jealous of your attention.

What You Can Do:

* In order to prepare your pet for the new member of your family, consider inviting friends with babies and children to visit prior to the arrival of your baby. This will allow you to see how your pet reacts to children while you are not distracted by your own child and have both hands free to intervene if a problem arises.

* Contact your veterinarian or visit on-line resource centers for information on this subject. Many on-line resources offer species- and breed-specific information.

* Slowly introduce your pet to your newborn. Speak to your veterinarian about the best approach for bringing your pet and baby together.

* Make a point of giving your pet lots of attention after you bring the baby home, and make an effort to keep your pet's schedule intact. If you believe that you and your partner will not have time to walk your pet as needed, arrange for a family member or neighbor's older child to walk your pet for you. If possible, make these arrangements prior to the arrival of your baby.

* Animals of certain breeds tend to be family friendly, while others tend to be more aggressive. However, a docile animal may become surprisingly dangerous very quickly, and an animal of a purportedly vicious breed may turn out to be a wonderful companion to your baby. Be alert to your pet's behavior. If you have any doubts at all, don't leave your pet alone with your baby.

* Encourage your partner and everyone else who will be around your baby to wash their hands after touching your pet.

When to Get More Help:

If your pet develops behavior problems after you bring your baby home, don't hesitate to seek the help of your veterinarian or an animal trainer.

Visitors

The Facts:

When you bring your new baby home, many people will want to meet your baby, visit you and your partner, and wish your new family well. Visitors are an unavoidable—and wonderful—aspect of this time in your life. The presence and congratulations of friends and family can make the arrival of a new baby even more joyful. Your job as the new father is to manage visits so that they continue to help—not hinder—your partner's recovery and transition to new parenthood.

What You Can Do:

* Sit down with your partner before the baby is born and make a strict visiting-hours schedule. Adjust the schedule if necessary once you bring the baby home.

* Consider recording an outgoing answering machine or voice-mail message on your telephone informing callers of the happy news and letting them know that the new father will be returning calls as soon as possible. Having recorded this message, allow the answering machine or voice mail to take all calls during the first few days or weeks.

* After you bring the baby home, help your partner manage the visiting schedule. Allow your partner to sleep and rest by fielding phone calls and knocks on the door. Often you will have to play "bouncer" and gently turn people away, asking them to come back at another time.

* If your friends and relatives have a habit of dropping in unannounced, consider putting a sign on your front door explaining, "We'd love to see you, but mother and baby are resting at the moment! Please call to arrange a more convenient visiting time."

* When friends and family offer to pay you a short visit during the day, consider how they can be helpful to you. When they ask what they can bring, ask them to stop by a market on their way and pick up whatever grocery items you need. Similarly, ask them to help set the table, hold the baby while your partner bathes, or assist in some other way.

* If your partner feels well and would prefer to get out of the house, suggest that a visit take place at a local park or other location outside your home. Visitors should not force you and your partner to entertain them in your home!

* If your or your partner's relationship with a particular family member is strained, suggest that visits with that person take place in a neutral location or at his or her home (rather than at yours), allowing you to control the length of the visits.

* Help your partner bring short visits to a close by politely indicating that it is time for mother or baby to nap or feed.

* As well-wishers bring or send gifts, keep a running list of the gifts received and the names of the givers. Help your partner by writing and sending thank-you notes. Although this may seem like a trivial task, the job of writing thank-you notes can seem overwhelming to a tired new mom, and knowing that her partner is keeping track of who sent which gifts can help her relax.

* Carefully consider the offers of long-term visitors who would like to come and stay. Will they be helpful to your new family, or will they simply create additional housework and require entertaining when you should be focusing on your baby and partner?

* On the other hand, certain long-term visitors can provide invaluable help. Having a relative help with the housework or child care can be a lifesaver to exhausted and overwhelmed parents. Before your baby is born, ask family members whether they might be able to stay with you if you require emergency help with housework or with the newborn. Prepare these family members for the fact that you may ask them to leave earlier than expected if you are blessed with an easy baby and you and your partner feel ready to go it alone. Show your gratitude by presenting helpers with thank-you gifts and offers to do similar favors for them in the future.

When to Get More Help:

If the visitors in your home create more chaos than comfort and you feel awkward turning friends and relatives away, ask a family member or friend to contact potential visitors and give them an update. This person can politely explain that your new family requires a few weeks to regroup before resuming your social schedule.

10 LIFE AFTER DELIVERY

Finding Time for Your Relationship

The Facts:

In choosing to have a baby, you and your partner have expanded your family as part of your commitment to your long-term relationship. Unfortunately, despite the best of intentions, a couple's decision to expand their family sometimes becomes the first step toward destroying that loving relationship.

? How can this be? Many couples put so much emphasis on the needs of their children and are so stressed by the responsibilities of parenthood that they forgo many of the basic activities and feelings that brought and kept them together—attention, intimacy, enthusiasm, and patience for each other. They lose sight of the fact that focusing on their children is not the same as focusing on each other. One of the best things you and your partner can do for your newborn is to continue to nurture the relationship between you. In doing so you will ensure that your baby will benefit from having parents who love each other.

What You Can Do:

* In order to maintain any semblance of a relationship, your partner must get enough sleep. A sleep-deprived woman will not have any energy available for her baby or for you. See "Sleep Deprivation & Insomnia" (page 76) and "A Parent's Guide to Adjusting to New Sleep Patterns" (page 228) for information on how you can assist your partner in getting more rest.

* Despite the overwhelming nature of your new reality, make efforts to continue the important activities of your old reality together. Prior to the arrival of your baby, sit down with your partner and talk about how you may be able to do this.

* When you spend time with your partner, make an effort to converse about a variety of subjects besides the baby—her health, her day, her friends and coworkers. Simply bringing up subjects that have nothing to do with the child will draw out your partner and encourage a return to the relationship you enjoyed prior to the arrival of your child.

* Include conversations with your partner in your work day. If possible, take a few minutes to call her, inquire about how she is doing, and exchange an intimate word. Treat her as if she were still your girlfriend. Flirt. Court her. If a few moments spent kidding around can reawaken a playfulness between you, then why not?

* Help your partner make time in her schedule for intimacy. Work as a team. Help her arrange time for breast pumping, child care, or anything else she requires in order to spend time together as a couple. Never make her feel that she must choose between you and the baby. Help her see how—together—you can make time for both.

* Your partner will be more likely to feel sexy and enthusiastic about spending a romantic evening with you if she is rested and knows that her baby is safe. If you would like to reintroduce intimacy into your relationship, take it upon yourself to help your wife get some rest and some personal time, despite your busy work schedule, new responsibilities, and worries. Care for the baby, or have someone else do so, in order to give your partner an opportunity to catch up on *at least* a few nights' sleep and bathe and groom herself leisurely. If you can arrange for a trusted hired helper, relative, or friend to babysit, invite your well-rested and groomed partner out on a date.

Getting a break from Diaper Central and having a romantic dinner out may just help to get her in the mood.

* Recruit a caregiver or extended family member to babysit on a regular basis so that you and your partner can go out alone. Doing this early on will prevent you from developing "baby-sitter paranoia" that prevents many parents from having *any* time alone without their kids for months on end.

* If you feel uncomfortable being intimate with your partner due to the way her body looks following delivery, keep in mind that her new appearance is temporary. See chapter 9, "Resuming Your Life Together" in this guidebook for more information.

* Be flexible. If you are accustomed to a steady "feeding sched-ule" of sex, you must be willing to alter your expectations. Think about different times of day, places, and methods. Also, realize that the rhythm of your intimacy may change—just when you finally have some time together, your baby may begin to cry. Resist the urge to make your partner feel guilty for getting up to soothe the baby.

* Make every effort to be alone with your partner. Call in favors and utilize the suggestions given in "Managing Child Care with the Help of Your Extended 'Family'" (page 240).

* Be understanding. Have a sense of humor. Be creative and make rebuilding your sex life something you do together. It may be different than before, but it can still be great.

When to Get More Help:

Reestablishing the intimacy between you is one of the most important things you can do to ensure that you maintain a happy and healthy family. If either of you is dissatisfied with your intimate relationship, discuss your concerns as soon as possible and contact a family therapist for assistance.

Resuming Your Sex Life

The Facts:

New mothers should not have sexual intercourse after delivery for at least three to four weeks. For the first few weeks, regardless of whether they delivered vaginally or by C-section, the cervix (the barrier between the vagina and the uterus) is open and prone to infection. In addition, new mothers experience heavy bleeding for the first two weeks following delivery. Intercourse can also be painful for new mothers due to vaginal bruising, an episiotomy cut, or tearing during the birth, for approximately six weeks.

Pain and discomfort during intercourse are exacerbated by a drop in estrogen after delivery that causes the vaginal walls to become less elastic and unlubricated. And many new mothers suffer from hemorrhoids. Add the shock of sleep deprivation, a daunting sense of new responsibility, and a changed body image, on top of a decreased level of estrogen production following delivery (one of the hormones responsible for women's sexual feelings), and a new mother will feel decidedly unsexy.

Meanwhile, the new father, who has not undergone the same physical and emotional changes his partner has, is eager to rekindle his love life and reconnect with his partner as they enter this phase of life together. In general, male partners will be ready for renewed intimacy before their female partners are. So how can these differing desires be reconciled?

This section focuses on providing tools for bringing a couple back together following the necessary physical separation after delivery. Maintaining a healthy relationship involves restoring the sexual activity that you enjoyed as a couple as soon as is practical. In addition, anecdotal evidence suggests that women who resume their sexual relationship with their partner are more motivated to lose weight, eat right, and be active and are less likely to feel isolated and depressed.

What You Can Do:

* Make physical reconnection with your partner a priority. Set aside time to be together, just as you make time to do other necessary things. Think of maintaining your physical intimacy with your partner and the reawakening of your sexuality as essential elements in building a happy, intact family.

* Once your perineum and vagina are completely healed, the sooner you resume sexual activity, the less physically uncomfortable the transition will be.

* If you feel unsexy after your delivery, making an effort to get back into the intimate swing of things may start up your engine again. Give it a try, even if the intimacy does not include intercourse; just being physically close may help.

* For six weeks following C-section, refrain from using the missionary position in order to protect the surgical incision.

* If your vaginal walls feel dry, ask your partner to pick up one of several over-the-counter glycerin-and-water-based lubricants, such as Astroglide and K-Y Jelly, available at your pharmacy. Alternatively, address vaginal dryness and lack of elasticity by using a natural estrogen cream that is safe for use when breastfeeding. See "Low or No Vaginal Lubrication & Elasticity" (page 158) for more information.

* To a certain extent, breastfeeding is a natural contraceptive, since it often delays ovulation for at least a few months after childbirth. So if you have unprotected sex between six weeks and three months after giving birth, you will probably not conceive. However, just in case you ovulate earlier than expected, it's a good idea to use birth control if you are not ready to get pregnant again.

* Be creative. Sometimes, in order to spend intimate time with your partner *and* know that your baby is safe, you will need to make love while your baby sleeps in the same room—or in the same bed—with you. Alternatively, there's no reason to limit your time together to the bed. Be flexible about location, time, and ways of sharing intimacy and satisfying sexual desire.

FOR THE NEW FATHER:

* During her pregnancy if you suspect that you will later have negative feelings associated with seeing the baby exit from your partner's vagina, request that you remain by your partner's head during the pushing stage of labor. Some men feel disturbed by the image of her vagina during delivery or by the appearance of her vagina after delivery. (In fact, it may be swollen and appear injured due to bloody discharge and her episiotomy cut or tears.) But rest assured that, within six weeks, the area will look and feel nearly the same as it did prior to the birth. See "Loss of Urinary or Vaginal Control" (page 155) for more information if her vagina does not return to the way it looked before.

* Your partner will be more likely to feel sexy and enthusiastic about spending a romantic evening with you if she is rested and knows that her baby is safe. If you would like to reintroduce intimacy into your relationship, take it upon yourself to help your wife get some rest and some personal time, despite your busy work schedule, new responsibilities, and worries. Care for the baby, or have someone else do so, in order to give your partner an opportunity to catch up on *at least* a few nights' sleep and bathe and groom herself leisurely. If you can arrange for a trusted hired helper, relative, or friend to babysit, invite your well-rested and groomed partner out on a date.

Getting a break from Diaper Central and having a romantic dinner out may just help to get her in the mood.

* In general, help your partner make time in her schedule for intimacy. Work as a team. Help her arrange time for breast pumping, child care, or anything else she requires in order to spend time together as a couple. Never make her feel that she must choose between you and the baby. Help her see how—together—you can make time for both.

* Just as a new mother must be flexible and creative regarding her sexuality, you must also be. If you are accustomed to a steady "feeding schedule" of sex, you must be willing to alter your expectations. Think about different times of day, places, and methods. Also, realize that the rhythm of your intimacy may change—just when you finally have some time together, your baby may begin to cry. Resist the urge to make your partner feel guilty for getting up to soothe the baby.

* Finally, be understanding. Have a sense of humor. Be creative and make rebuilding your sex life something you do together. It may be different than before, but it can still be great.

When to Get More Help:

If your partner experiences pain during intercourse after waiting at least six weeks following delivery, encourage her to consult her physician regarding lubricants and other options. If she still experiences pain even with the lubricant, it is appropriate to contact her physician for an evaluation. It may be that her the tears or cuts she sustained during delivery were sewn too tightly, or that her scar tissue is not healing properly.

If your partner complains that her sex drive is not what it was prior to delivery, explore with your partner the wide variety of nutritional remedies and hormones that may enhance her sexual desire. To find out about these remedies, consult an OB/GYN who specializes in nutritional medicine.

Finding Time for You & Your Partner to Be Active

The Facts:

One of the most important things a new mother can do following her delivery is to get back into her normal exercise routine. The same can be said of a new father. Encouraging each other to resume or begin personal exercise programs—besides spending time being active together—is an excellent way to hold on to a piece of the life you enjoyed prior to the arrival of your baby.

What You Can Do:

* See "Exercise & Activity after Vaginal Delivery" (page 153) and "Exercise & Activity after C-Section" (page 52) for specific information on the restrictions on activity following delivery.

* Help your partner introduce an exercise program into her daily schedule as early as possible. Even if she is only able to engage in light walking while pushing a stroller, encourage her to make time every day for getting out and exercising. After all, exercise can be an important time to think, plan, and help maintain one's sanity during a challenging time.

* Plan active outings together. Walking or hiking together with your baby in a baby carrier—even if only to your local shopping mall—is an excellent way to start becoming active and an even better way to spend time together.

* If your baby rises early, consider getting up with him, throwing on comfortable shoes, and going out for a morning walk. After all, if you have to be awake in the early-morning hours, why not make that time productive? Alternatively, if *you* wake early and your baby is still asleep, don't be afraid to wake her (and feed her) and put her into her baby carrier or stroller for a walk.

* When you return from work, grab your partner's hand and your baby and take them both out for a romantic stroll.

* A rigid exercise schedule that does not take into account your baby's and partner's needs can be very destructive, both to your exercise routine and to your relationship with your partner. If you have a standing 6:00 a.m. appointment with a trainer or workout buddy and your partner and baby need you at that time, your workout routine is likely to create tension between you and your partner. Be flexible for the first six or so months of your baby's life, and *always* take into account the needs of your family.

When to Get More Help:

Exercise and activity should be a priority. If you and your partner are still unable to find *any* time for activity two months into your baby's life, ask friends and family members to help you by watching the baby while you exercise either together or separately.

Finding Time for Your Social Life

The Facts:

Having a child is not a reason to disrupt one's social life. Despite the best intentions, many couples who have a child are rarely (or never) seen again by their friends. They seem to live in a constant state of emergency that prevents them from making social plans in advance, committing to social functions and trips, and generally enjoying the company of their friends. Needless to say, this is not a healthy or enjoyable way of living.

Babies need parents who take care of themselves, which includes getting enough rest, eating a healthy diet, exercising, and socializing. In light of this, try to maintain a scaled-down version of your pre-baby social schedule.

What You Can Do:

* Push yourselves to reemerge from your baby-induced social hiatus by scheduling social plans with friends. By setting up these meetings ahead of time, you will force yourselves to make arrangements (e.g., child care) that will allow you to meet these commitments.

* If your baby is generally peaceful and tends to sleep when you take him out, you may decide to take your baby with you, as long as your friends do not mind. But be considerate of your friends—a couple who have gone to great lengths to hire a babysitter for their own children so that they can have a grown-ups' dinner out may not be pleased if you bring your active baby along.

* Recruit a caregiver or extended family member to babysit on a regular basis so that you and your partner can go out alone. Doing this early on will prevent you from developing

"babysitter paranoia" that prevents many parents from having *any* time alone without their kids for months on end.

* If you cannot arrange for child care, consider inviting friends to your house. Order dinner in or host a potluck (and accept your friends' help with cleanup!). Good friends will be happy to help with dinner and the dishes if it gives them an opportunity to see you.

* Some couples find that their friends who do not have children suddenly lose interest in socializing with them. Often this is because the new parents' schedule is less conducive to the types of social activities they engaged in before, but it may also be that the couple without children feel that they have little to say to new parents consumed by the small wonders of new parenthood. They fear that they simply can't relate. When you socialize with these friends, consider promising to talk about your baby only when asked. (This will also give you a short vacation from your new-baby universe.)

* You and your partner may benefit from befriending couples who also have a new baby. Accept invitations to be introduced to friends of friends with new babies and keep your eyes open at the park or at any infant-care or childbirth preparation classes you attend. Introduce yourselves to the couples who seem friendly and interesting and see if you hit it off.

When to Get More Help:

If you and your partner find that you have not gone out alone or seen friends in an adult setting for more than three months, don't be shy—call up a trusted friend and ask him or her to babysit.

Glossary of Terms

Adrenal Gland
The gland that produces adrenaline, a hormone that is released in response to stress or danger and supplies the body with enough energy and stamina to get out of the stressful or dangerous situation.

Baby Blues
A mild form of depression and moodiness that may occur immediately after the delivery and last several months, and that is not severe enough to be classified as postpartum depression.

Breast Engorgement
A painful condition that arises when the breast accumulates too much milk, either due to delayed breastfeeding or an attempt to stop breastfeeding.

Colostrum
The substance produced and secreted by the breast in the first few days following delivery.

DHEA
A male hormone also found in women.

Diuretic
A food or medication that causes the body to release liquid via urination and perspiration.

Electrolytes
An essential substance found in minerals, such as sea salt, that is commonly added to sports drinks.

Episiotomy

A medical procedure in which the tissue between the vagina and the rectum is severed in order to prevent or reduce tearing during the pushing stage of labor.

Estradiol (E2)

One of the three forms of the female hormone estrogen.

Esteron (E1)

One of the three forms of the female hormone estrogen.

Estriol (E3)

One of the three forms of the female hormone estrogen.

Estrogen

A female hormone composed of three forms, esteron (E1), estradiol (E2), and estriol (E3).

First Stage Labor

The initial portion of labor during which a pregnant woman experiences contractions but does not yet begin to push.

Hemorrhoids

A painful inflammation of the veins around the rectum.

Homeopathic

A form of medication that is an alternative to traditional medication, based on a homeopathy system of treatment.

Homeopathy

A system of medical practice that treats a disease by the administration of minute doses of a remedy that would produce symptoms similar to those of the disease in a healthy person.

Hypoglycemia

A drop in blood sugar common in pregnancy, especially in the first trimester, but also in the first months following delivery, due to a new mother's tendency to skip meals.

Hypotension

A low blood-pressure condition associated with a drop in blood sugar.

Inverted Nipples

A condition wherein the nipples do not point outward, which may require a new mother to speak to a lactation consultant before and after the delivery of her baby, in order to avoid problems with breastfeeding.

Kegel Exercises

Exercises, performed by squeezing the vaginal muscles, designed to help strengthen these muscles before and after delivery.

Lactobacillus Acidophilus

A healthful bacteria found in unsweetened, unflavored dairy products, and in pill form, that can help the body fight infection.

Lactation Specialist or Lactation Consultant

A professional who helps pregnant women and new mothers identify the ideal manner in which to nurse their baby. Lactation classes are offered by most hospitals and many new-mother groups or may be given in one-on-one consultations.

Mastitis

An infection of the breasts.

Melatonin	The body's natural sleeping aid, produced when the body is exposed to darkness and quiet. When the body fails to produce enough melatonin, lack of sleep, fatigue, and exhaustion are likely. Supplements may be taken in pill form.
Postpartum	The period of time after delivery, generally regarded as the first six months to one year.
Pregnenolone	A hormone found in men and women.
Progesterone	A female hormone also found in men. Progesterone plays an especially important role in pregnancy.
Second Stage Labor	The more advanced stage of labor when a pregnant woman's cervix is fully dilated and she begins pushing.
Sutures	Stitches or other devices used by medical professionals to reattach skin and muscle tissue after a vaginal or C-section delivery.
Testosterone	A male hormone also found in women.
Thrush or Nipple Thrush	An infection that can occur in the baby's mouth or in the nipple, which may be transferred from one to the other.
Thyroid	A hormone found in men and women.

Thyroiditis

An infection of the gland that produces thyroid.

Varicose Veins

An inflammation of the veins in the legs and in the pelvic area.

Index

A

abdomen
changes in, 163–65
exercises for, 153–54, 156
acetaminophen, 49, 61, 62
acupuncture, 65, 69
Addison's disease, 95, 96, 98
adrenal gland exhaustion, 95–98,
177–78
adrenaline, 95, 177, 196–97, 200
alpha lipoic acid, 107
amino acids, 86–87
anal tears, 30–33
anemia, 41–42
ankles, swollen, 34–37
answering machine message, 244
antidepressants, 179, 203
antioxidants, 167
anxiety
effects of, 170
mild, 81–84
natural remedies for, 202, 203
postpartum depression dominated
by, 194–203
progesterone and, 102–3
arnica, 43, 49–50, 58
aspirin, 27, 61
attachment parenting, 225

B

baby
bonding with, 20–21
crying, 225
pets and, 242–43
preparing for arrival of, 20–21
size of, 155
sleep patterns of, 222–27
on social outings, 257
visitors and, 244–46
baby blues, 175, 176, 182–84
babysitting, 250, 257–58. See also
child care
back pain, 64–66

bassinets, 233
baths
after C-section, 46
sitz, 39
after vaginal delivery, 45–46
bills, paying, 236
birth control, 252
black cohosh, 109
bladder infections, 50–51
bleeding, 25–27
blood loss, 41–42
blood sugar, low, 106–8
blood vessels, broken, 43–44
breastfeeding. See also breast pumping; breasts; nipples
beginning, 112–15
benefits of, 112
breast size and, 118
as a choice, 112, 115, 144, 145
diet guidelines for, 149–50
disappointment with, 112–13
father's feelings about, 138–40
lactation specialists and, 113, 115,
121
milk production and, 121–22
as natural contraceptive, 252
pain medication and, 61
positions, 130
in public, 114, 135–37
stopping, 145–46
work and, 141–44
breast pumping, 114, 136, 141–44
breasts. See also nipples
engorgement of, 119–20
infected (mastitis), 131–32
massaging, 129
plugged ducts, 129–30
size of, 118
bromelain, 39, 50

C

caffeine, 160
calcium, 29, 83, 199, 209
carpal tunnel syndrome, 68–70
cats, 242–43

Notes: